TWENTIETH CENTURY INTERPRETATIONS

OF

# BILLY BUDD

TWENTIETH CENTURY INTERPRETATIONS
OF

# BILLY BUDD

*A Collection of Critical Essays*

Edited by

HOWARD P. VINCENT



Prentice-Hall, Inc. 

*Englewood Cliffs, N. J.*

C-13-084715-1; P-13-084707-0. *Library of Congress Catalog Card Number 76-133055.*
Printed in the United States of America.

Current printing (last number):
10 9 8 7 6 5 4 3 2 1

Prentice-Hall International, Inc. (*London*)
Prentice-Hall of Australia, Pty. Ltd. (*Sydney*)
Prentice-Hall of Canada, Ltd. (*Toronto*)
Prentice-Hall of India Private Limited (*New Delhi*)
Prentice-Hall of Japan, Inc. (*Tokyo*)

# Contents

TWENTIETH CENTURY INTERPRETATIONS

OF

# BILLY BUDD

# Introduction

## *by Howard P. Vincent*

Herman Melville was born in New York City on 1 August 1819. He died in the same city 28 September 1891. His life spanned a remarkable century, which he knew well from his own extraordinary travels to the far places of the world, and further, because, like Wordsworth's Newton, he "travelled strange seas of thought alone." In *Mardi,* Melville cried out, "Oh reader, I have chartless voyaged." *Billy Budd* is the culminating report of those lifelong wanderings.

Comfortably middle-class, Melville's parents united the New England tradition of the Melvilles with the Dutch patroon tradition of the Gansevoorts. When Melville was thirteen, his father in quick succession suffered bankruptcy, mental collapse, and death. The family was destitute, and the boys left school to take on jobs to support themselves and their mother. Herman tried several jobs, each of brief duration, including service on a merchant ship across the Atlantic. He went into the then American West on a trip to Galena, Illinois, in 1840. Soon after that he signed on the whaleship *Acushnet* to begin the three years of fabulous voyaging which became the foundation of his ultimate fame. He served on board three whaleships; he wandered in three island groups of Oceania: the Marquesas, the Society, and the Sandwich (Hawaiian); and he enlisted 17 August 1843, at Honolulu, in the United States Navy, serving on board the frigate *United States* for the fourteen-month voyage back home. Arriving in Boston in October 1844, Melville may have had but little money in his pocket and but few possessions in his duffle bag, but he had a wealth of memories far more valuable than a tourist's souvenirs.

For twelve years following his return home, Melville struggled to earn his living as a writer, a task in which he had a brief success before ultimate defeat. His first two books, *Typee* (1846) and *Omoo* (1847), were immensely successful. Melville's skillful account of exotic peoples and adventures in the Marquesas and Society Islands made him known as "the man who had lived among the cannibals." A third, more ambitious, book, *Mardi* (1848), failed with his public and, as he indicated, flattened his purse. Two subsequent travel books, *Redburn* (1849) and *White-Jacket* (1850), retrieved his popularity. His sixth book, *Moby-Dick* (1851), was his masterpiece, but the reception of that and two subsequent novels clearly demonstrated that writing was economically hazardous in America, particularly for a man with Melville's increasing family responsibilities. In due time he gave up writing as a career, finding a job at last in 1866 as an Inspector of Customs in the Port of New York. Despite the pressure of these labors, he continued to write, composing poems primarily for his own pleasure and concern. *Clarel* (1876), an 18,000-line narrative poem, was published at his uncle's expense and was scarcely noticed by critics. Melville's had become a voice whispering in the wilderness.

On the last day of the year 1885, Melville retired from his post as Inspector. His wife explained the action:

> For a year or so past he has found his duties too onerous for a man of his years, and at times of exhaustion, both mental and physical, he has been on the point of giving it up, but recovering a little, has held on, very naturally anxious to do so, for many reasons—This month was a good turning-point, completing 19 years of faithful service, during which there was not a single complaint against him—So he retires honorably of his own accord—He has a great deal [of] unfinished work at his desk which will give him occupation, which together with his love of books will prevent time from hanging heavy on his hands—and I hope he will get into a more quiet frame of mind, exempt from the daily invitation of over work—

The month "was a good turning-point" for another reason: Mrs. Melville had recently received a legacy which made retirement financially possible.

"Retirement" is perhaps the wrong term; "change of activity" would be better. The productivity of Melville in his last six years, retired, was remarkable: two volumes of published verse, one volume arranged for publication but not printed, and one novel composed. Quality kept pace with quantity. Melville's great flowering in his old age was of a kind, and indeed, with *Billy Budd,* of a radiance comparable to the rejuvenescence we discern in the late paintings of Titian, in the late songs of Richard Strauss, or the last quartets of Beethoven, in Sophocles' *Oedipus at Colonus*—visual, verbal, and tonal works in which a lifetime of rich experience and of mastered technique combine for final statements like profound benedictions addressed to an absurd and meaningless universe.

Undoubtedly, however, Melville's first days at his desk must have been housecleaning, an unwitting readying of his papers and of himself for the remarkable days ahead. Like Candide long before him, Melville cultivated his garden, an image which he himself used in several forms when talking about his literary labors. Very quickly, he felt intensifying within himself a renewed poetic creativeness, finding renewed power in a process that Robert Duncan has well described:

> The design of a poem
> constantly
> under reconstruction,
> changing, pusht forward;
> alternations of sound, sensations;
> the mind dance
> wherein thot shows its pattern:
> a proposition
> in movement.

The "great heap [of] unfinished work at his desk which will give him occupation" was a heap of poems composed or started by Melville during the decades following *The Confidence-Man* (1857). From this heap he first arranged a collection, *John Marr and Other Sailors* (1888), printed in an edition of twenty-five copies for distribution to friends.

The poems of *John Marr*—and later, of *Timoleon* (1891)—were a remarkable instance of *recherche du temps perdu,* Melville's mind moving back to his years of voyaging throughout the Polynesian triangle and in the Mediterranean to the Holy Land. And in all, there is throughout the persistent memory of the sea itself, Melville's most powerful, prevalent, and creative symbol. Toward that sea, at once cruel and beautiful, Melville now felt benign, and in one short poem, which he called a "pebble," he wrote: "Healed of my hurt, I laud the inhuman Sea."

*John Marr* has special interest for us, especially the four poems that deal with John Marr, Bridegroom Dick, Tom Deadlight, and Jack Roy, who in their old age ramble reminiscently about their seafaring past. Freely constructed, these poems vary their structure with occasional bridges of prose, suggesting that Melville was instinctively moving toward a full-scale use of prose fiction, in which he had once shown his mastery and with which he had won his former fame. The prose of *Billy Budd* had its origins in these arrangements for *John Marr.* A brief ballad, "Billy in the Darbies," was certainly intended for the little volume. The original version, canceled, described an old sailor named Billy, waiting the night out in the brig before his execution at dawn for mutiny.

Obviously Melville sensed possibilities, needs, for development of mere hints, even omissions, in "Billy in the Darbies." Starting with a thirty-two line ballad, Melville began a process of circling expansion reminiscent of the days of *Moby-Dick* and *Pierre.* Like James Joyce deliberately reworking a clear paragraph of *Finnegan's Wake* to render a complex compression of bewildering pluralistic materials, Melville, in time, enlarged his simple ballad into a disturbing study of the "mystery of iniquity." Thus, a simple story grew, was transformed, gained moral grandeur, as long before the simple hunt for the sperm whale had expanded in drastic revision to the grandeurs of *Moby-Dick*.

Interestingly, Melville logged his voyage through the composition of *Billy Budd*: First on the manuscript, "Friday Nov. 16, 1888. Began." Four months later, "Revise—began March 2d 1889." And last, "End of Book/April 19th/1891." Thus, tersely, we have the course of the book from a single canceled page to 351 confusing pages of drafts.

A proper study of the slow creation, over three years, of *Billy Budd* would demand a book. This will be written some day, but to write it will not be easy; rude hands must tear filiations that are cobweb in texture. To study how a book is put together is at times as hard, as exasperating, and as violating as the author's own composing. And that was difficult, always, for Melville, who said while he was writing *Moby-Dick*:

> Taking a book off the brain is akin to the ticklish & dangerous business of taking an old painting off a panel—you have to scrape off the whole brain in order to get at it with safety.

The *Billy Budd* scrapings of Melville's brain lie in the 351 pages of manuscript now in the Houghton Library at Harvard. The manuscript is an object of literary pilgrimage, of course, and it has been an object of much study. Early readings of the pages were faulty because the editors were unable to cope with Melville's notoriously bad handwriting and with the twistings and windings of his revisions toward a final form. The stages of Melville's work have now been fully described by Hayford and Sealts in their great edition of *Billy Budd,* from which it is well to read of Melville's progress:

> In three main phases he had introduced in turn the three main characters: first Billy, then Claggart, and finally Vere. As the focus of his attention shifted from one to another of these three principals, the plot and thematic emphasis of the expanding novel underwent consequent modifications within each main phase. Just where the emphasis finally lay in the not altogether finished story as he left it is, in essence, the issue that has engaged and divided the critics of *Billy Budd*.

This simplified statement by Hayford and Sealts is in accord with what we know of the author's practices in previous books. *Moby-Dick* itself was, according to Melville, a similar creative exfoliating, a pushing out from a simple center to include a complex world of experience.

The chaotic state of the manuscript, with its bewildering corrections, cancelations, starts, and shiftings, has inclined some critics of *Billy Budd* to see in the book, as it is now printed, a parallel confusion. They suggest that Melville was trapped in his writing because he was trapped in uncertainty, baffled by the moral labyrinths wherein both pen and spirit wandered. Melville, they point out, spent more than three years composing a 75-page—story? novella? novel?—whereas previously he had written novels eight times its length in but half the time, or less. They see, then, the manuscript as a metaphor of Melville's mind. They forget that Melville was an old man, feeble in health, working also on a book of poems, *Timoleon* (1891), and under no pressure to publish. He was cultivating his garden in retirement, not undertaking a farmer's job from which to earn his livelihood.

A single, judicially satisfying answer as to whether or not *Billy Budd* was ever finished will probably never be reached. Mrs. Melville said that it was "unfinished." From her point of view, and allowing for her kind of responsibility to the manuscript, it was; she was the amanuensis, not the author, and to her, of course, it was unfinished in that it needed much recopying, ordering of pages, and last-minute revisions before it was sent off to the printer.

Melville himself apparently considered the story finished. At least he wrote at the end of the manuscript. "End of book/April 19th/1891." Since he scrupulously logged the course of the manuscript from beginning through revision and now at conclusion, his entries must be respected. End means end, for which "finished" is normally a synonym. Possibly, of course, he meant by "end" that at this spot the plot of his story ended and that he would in time go back over the whole thing to revise it, extend it, clarify it, render it as a fable comprehensible to babes.

It is of course absurd to argue the unfinished nature of *Billy Budd* from the fact that it is full of ambiguities. Melville was a connoisseur of ambiguities, mystifications, riddles. *Mardi* (1848) he had admitted to be a huge riddle, which he felt that only Time might solve, and its riddlings delighted Hawthorne, himself a master-riddler. *Moby-Dick* (1851) was equally, if more subtly and successfully, a riddle book. Melville admitted it in interpreting the Spouter-Inn painting as a headache. Throughout *Pierre* (1853), too, the hero struggles with manuscripts frenetically (he is Thomas Wolfe prefigured), and not only did Melville give his book the full title of *Pierre or The Ambiguities* (1853), but the word ambiguity rings throughout the novel like an iterative chime. So now, more than thirty years later, Melville shows himself still an unrepentant devotee of the cryptic. He openly warns his readers:

> X———is a nut not to be cracked by the tap of a lady's fan. . . . [To] try and get into X———enter his labyrinth and get out again, without

a clue from some other source than what is known as "knowledge of the world"—that were hardly possible, at least for me.

At least for critics, too. What is gathered in this volume are some of the more effective or more interesting fan taps.

Among the many materials stirring in Melville's mind to create *Billy Budd* were memories of a man, a book, and an event.

First was John J. Chase, Melville's shipmate on board the frigate *United States,* transformed into the flamboyant Jack Chase of *White-Jacket,* and the man to whom, forty years later, Melville dedicated his ultimate creation. Jack Chase is the prototype for Billy Budd, but with significant differences, especially in speech, since the rhetorical cascades of Jack Chase contrast strikingly with the stuttering of young Billy.

A second influence was *White-Jacket,* Melville's detailed account of life on board a man-of-war (the *United States* of fact becoming the *Neversink* of fiction), the same ship–world stage, and metaphor, on which Billy Budd's tragedy is enacted. Jack Chase is in the book, as is a villain named Bland, a quickly drawn sketch from which Claggart would develop. Furthermore, moral and ethical problems strongly drawn in *Billy Budd* ricochet throughout the realistic trappings of *White-Jacket* to give even that comic–satiric work a serious and dark side.

The third source was the *Somers* mutiny (1842) in the United States Navy, in which Captain Mackenzie (subtilized and symbolized into Vere) ordered the hanging on board ship of three mutineers, an arbitrary and unexpected decision which split the United States into two camps and which still remains a divisive problem in our history. For Melville it had a special significance not only because his cousin, Guert Gansevoort, was a lieutenant on board the *Somers* at the time and was closely involved with the guarding and the hanging of the mutineers, but also because Melville himself had twice symbolically mutinied on board whaleships.

From these principal strands was woven the complex and subtle fabric of *Billy Budd.*

*Billy Budd* is generally first perceived by the reader, and often approached by the critic, as a fable or morality play, with most of our attention directed to the interplay of meanings as each of the three central characters steps forward to dominate the stage. Written largely from private need on Melville's part, as private as his privately printed poems, *Billy Budd* has a subtle quality which moves us to circling reflections. This privateness is also part of the seeming simplicity of the work, the deceptive simplicity one gets in the words of a wise old man whose gentle voice softens stern truth. Had *Billy Budd* been written with the book-buying world uppermost in Melville's mind, it would have been, health permitting, a far different book in its details. Melville would have fleshed out the story with shipboard life as he had once done, without much story, in *White-Jacket.* It would have been a more graspable book. Now, not caring to entertain the world, he could softly utter his last, closely considered words. He could be, had to be, brief and simple. Ultimate wisdom is never simple, no matter how elementary the syntax, and its condensations demand from the reader a sophistication and a seriousness equivalent to that of the writer. Take one great simplicity which echoes in men's minds: "Men must endure their going hence, even as their coming hither. Ripeness is all." That surely is simple and clear, and yet how shifting is its sense as one reads the sentences in successive years, as words like "endure," "going," "coming," and "Ripeness" are placed beneath the microscopic lens of an intensely lived life. What child mind can ever dimly sense the terror and absoluteness of Lear's great recognition: "Never, never, never, never, never," the fivefold repetition with its object—death?

*Billy Budd,* however, has been most studied for its meanings and not for its manner. It is effective not because it might give us a stock of Polonian platitudes, but because it is written well. Melville was an artist and not just a sailor–philosopher blundering into cracker-barrel insights. To see how a sailor once more, for a last time, achieved artistic excellence would be an illuminating genetic study, a lesson in composition. As Emerson said, it is not the What that matters but the How.

A study of the stylistics should notice Melville's cunning in the names of his characters. In this strategy he and other writers of the time had the illustrious example of Charles Dickens, the names of whose characters are worth chapters of description. One thinks randomly of Uriah Heep, Micawber, the Cheeryble brothers, Pecksniff, and Gradgrind. With Melville a similar pleasure comes from reading "Bartleby," where minor characters like Ginger Nuts, Turkey, and Nippers are labeled with comic skill, and where the name of Bartleby achieves poetic genius, teasing the reader's mind forever. Elsewhere and earlier Melville had balanced tantalizingly between realism and allegorical suggestion, as in Wellingborough Redburn. The ship's list of the *Pequod* is masterly in this way.

In *Billy Budd* Melville retained his old skill. His hero, Billy, has the simplest and commonest of nicknames; only Jack would have been as appropriate for a sailor, but Billy serves well in its representative character, and has the further advantage of alliteration with "Budd." Budd is as rare as Billy is common, and this is a felicitous polarization. Budd himself is a rare person. His beautiful innocence is summed up in the bud image. It is not, however, only in its indication of meaning that "Budd" serves well; it is subtle in its spelling. The two *d*'s suggest delicately the fundamental stammer which is Billy's tragic limitation.

Claggart is in every way, in name as well as in person, the opposite of Billy Budd. "Claggart" is a clanging and grinding sound; its gutturals snarl and cough in contrast to "Billy Budd," where the labial *b*'s suggest a caress and a kiss. "Claggart" has its flat first syllable, its grating second; "Billy Budd" has a pleasant lilt with its dancing dactyl followed by the sharp yet clean monosyllable of the last name. "Claggart" has ugly associations in its echoes: *braggart, haggard, ragged, staggered, laggard, slacker, lack, clog, clang, clangor, anger, angered, girt, guard, grr, ger* (Indo-European, "to cry," and a root in words like *crow* and *crane*), and *grate.* There is the rural English word *claggen* meaning "to daub with mud," the Danish *Klagge, "mud."* Such meanings implicit in the tonality of "Claggart" cling to his person within the story.

Vere is also opposed to Claggart in sound and sense. Whereas both Billy Budd and Claggart have names but have no certainly known backgrounds, their pasts shrouded in mystery and gossip, Captain Vere is solidly centered in the story and in a distinguished, long-lived culture. Vere is an honorable name in English history, as Melville stresses, standing for an aristocratic tradition, the role of authority, and for paternal consideration and kindness. "Vere" also suggests the Latin word for "truth," *verus,* while the Latin *vir* may suggest Vere's "power" or "energy." His name also suggests "very," which is an intensive. It is Captain Vere who insists on the fulfillment of the orders which he has sworn to serve. He is a very "very" man.

Similarly, but less extensively, a study of the minor names might yield interesting reflections (for mirror-glintings is what they are), with Old Dansker, Red Whiskers, and Squeak much in the Dickensian comic manner. They are, however, metaphors of description, as quickly grasped as the sense of the characters themselves.

A possible semibiographical, symbolic interpretation of the composition of *Billy Budd* (not of the book itself) is suggested by Melville's motivation for writing, and then canceling, the first draft of "Billy in the Darbies." The early draft of the poem, with its description of an old sailor in the brig on mutiny charges, waiting to die, was Melville's projection of his own nineteen years of Customs servitude, of his literary hanging, by neglect, by the American reading public and by ill-fate, and of his own long-felt, ill-repressed mutiny against the ship of the world. He who had twice fled whaleships—and such flights were a form of mutinous protest against those ship worlds—and who had felt that to tell the truth, as a writer, was itself a form of mutiny against the "crested lies of Mardi"—such a man would have seen his artless verse sketch as a significant doodling which exposed his own unconscious rebellion and summed up much of his hidden life. So Melville canceled the draft, not because he feared exposure (for who would find him out?), but because he wanted further to expose, or to develop, the essential defiance implicit in the verses. In due time, over several years, the subsequent drafts of the completing manuscript became an apt metaphor for Melville's own creative being, for his final and triumphant freedom.

A twentieth century poet has sensed this and has beautifully written about this late Melville that he at last "sailed into an extraordinary mildness" (see "Herman Melville," reprinted on pp. 89–92 of this volume). Auden then added, "he sat down and wrote a poem." One must insist on the mildness as well as admire the resultant poem. He, who would soon abjure all rough magic, had, like Prospero (and thus like Shakespeare), "Some heavenly music, which even now I do, / To work mine end upon their senses." Critics may disagree about exactly what the "end" is meant to be, but certainly it is above all a wonderful sense of ending. *Nunc dimittis.*

While writing *Billy Budd,* Melville was clearly condemned by Time itself to his imminent death, felt in his blood and in his bones. Against this encroaching catastrophe, Melville fought with the chief resource at his command, his pen, challenging the mortality of the flesh with the immortality of art. In his final words, he who had stammered, he felt, through many years of writing (for what was an unreading public but a sign of his non-communication, his stammer?), could now speak out loud and clear, stammer vanished, to assert in simplicity what John Keats (so like Melville in many insights) had termed "the holiness of the heart's affections."

The original sketch of "Billy in the Darbies" was a parable of Melville's—and, indeed, man's—long-caged condition. With the cancelation of that draft and with the several enlarging drafts of the extended story, and with the revised "Billy in the Darbies" now triumphantly placed as the conclusion, the poetic crown—now, with all this achieved, it may be seen by us as a single, flowing action, a larger and more profound parable of the emergent freedom which retirement, return to his desk, and writing brought to Melville the man. Through his art he found his final freedom.

Auden was, of course, right. Melville did sail into an "extraordinary mildness." Many men, to be sure, sail into an ordinary mildness but with muteness or mumbling as a consequence, and with the normal, old-age sapping of energies, the drying-up of calcium salts in the body. Melville's was an "extraordinary mildness" because it was *not* passive resignation common to and expected from old men; it was instead a wonderful creative renewal.

Again Auden said it well: "For now he was awake and knew / No one is ever spared except in dreams." Once again, Melville was awake to the woe and the wonder of the world, even of Society, wicked though he knew it to be. He who had, through Father Mapple, celebrated the woe and the delight of the world re-echoed that complex but fundamental affirmation. The poets, Emerson said, are the liberating gods, but the most important of their liberations is their own. This Melville achieved in *Billy Budd,* and his compositional struggle is emblematic of his psychological and artistic triumph.

## PART ONE

### *Interpretations*

# Melville's Testament of Acceptance

### *by E. L. Grant Watson*

Melville finished the short novel, *Billy Budd,* five months before his death in 1891. It was not published until 1924, when it was included in the Constable edition of 750 copies. No other printing has yet appeared.

The style of this product of Melville's last years is strikingly different from the exuberant and highly-colored prose of that great period of more ardent creation (1850 to 1852) which produced *Mardi, Moby-Dick,* and *Pierre.* Though it lacks that fine extravagance of the earlier books, which laid on the color with prodigality, *Billy Budd* is as rich, or even richer, in Melville's peculiar and elaborate symbolism; and this symbolism becomes all the more effective for being presented in a dry and objective manner. The fine flourishes, the purple patches, which scintillate brilliantly in *Moby-Dick,* and the deep sombre melancholy of *Pierre* are not here. The grandiloquence of youth which tempted Stevenson's very partial appreciation is here transformed into the dignity of an achieved detachment. The story develops simply, always unhurried, yet never lagging. Each character is described with the patience which the complex intention of the theme demands—the color of the eyes, the clothes, the complexion, the color of the skin, of the blood under the skin, the past, the present—these are hints at a deep and solemn purpose, one no less ambitious than to portray those ambiguities of good and evil as the mutually dependant opposites, between which the world of realization finds its being.

The title *Billy Budd* is not without significance, and would strike some readers in its crude simplicity as proof that Melville was lacking in a sense of humor. How could any man, they would argue, write a tragedy and call it *Billy Budd*? But a sense of humor, like almost everything else, is relative. Melville certainly lacked it in the crude form; but he was always conscious of those occasions when he might seem,

---

*"Melville's Testament of Acceptance" by E. L. Grant Watson. From* New England Quarterly *6 (June 1933): 319–27. Reprinted by permission of the publisher.*

to a superficial view, to be wanting it. He is particularly conscious of the obvious, but not in the obvious manner; and when he uses such a name as *Billy Budd* to set as the hub round which his own philosophy of life must revolve, he does so consciously, choosing the obvious to carry the transcendental. "I have ever found the plain things, the knottiest of all," he has written; and so he had made the simple man, the every-day Billy, the handsome sailor, the hero of a tragedy. Humor is appreciated most easily when larger things contract suddenly to smaller things—as when a man slips on a piece of orange-peel, thus converting his intention of going about his business to the abrupt act of falling on his back-side. Yet a more imaginative intelligence might, with a sense of humor just as true, see in this fall, the destiny of man, with full chorus of pities and ironic spirits. The easy contraction will seem to the sophisticated too facile to provoke a smile, a larger humor is found in the reverse process, namely in a filling in, in an exaggeration from the particular to the general. With such an added pinch of imagination, the obvious thing becomes the center of mystery. And so, with a sense of humor which perceived both the obvious and the peculiar quality of the name, Melville deliberately chose "Billy Budd." Moreover, he made the hero of this, his gospel story (as it might well be called), a foundling of uncertain parentage, whose "entire family was practically invested in himself."

It is a mistake for critics to try to tell stories which authors must have told better in their texts. The critic's function is rather to hint at what lies beneath—hidden, sometimes, under the surface. Melville called his story "an inside narrative," and though it deals with events stirring and exciting enough in themselves, it is yet more exciting because it deals with the relation of those principles which constitute life itself. A simple-mindedness unaffected by the shadow of doubt, a divine innocence and courage, which might suggest a Christ not yet conscious of His divinity, and a malice which has lost itself in the unconscious depths of mania—the very mystery of iniquity—these opposites here meet, and find their destiny. But Melville's theme is even larger. All the grim setting of the world is in the battleship *Indomitable*; war and threatened mutiny are the conditions of her existence. Injustice and inhumanity are implicit, yet Captain Vere, her commander, is the man who obeys the law, and yet understands the truth of the spirit. It is significant of Melville's development since the writing of *Moby-Dick* and *Pierre,* that he should create this naval captain—wholly pledged to the unnaturalness of that law, but sufficiently touched, at the same time, by the divine difference from ordinary sanity (he goes by the nickname of "Starry Vere"), as to live the truth *within* the law, and yet, in the cruel process of that very obedience, to redeem an innocent man from the bitterness of death imposed by the same law. A very different ending this from the despairing acts of dissolution which mark the conclusions of the three earlier books: *Mardi, Moby-Dick,* and *Pierre.*

Melville is no longer a rebel. It should be noted that Billy Budd has not, even under the severest provocation, any element of rebellion in him; he is too free a soul to need a quality which is a virtue only in slaves. His nature spontaneously accepts whatever may befall. When impressed from the merchant-ship, the *Rights of Man,* he makes no demur to the visiting lieutenant's order to get ready his things for trans-shipment. The crew of the merchant-ship are surprised and reproachful at his uncomplaining acquiescence. Once aboard the battleship, the young sailor begins to look around for the advantages of chance and adventure. Such simple power to accept gives him the buoyancy to override troubles and irritations which would check inferior natures.

Yet his complete unconsciousness of the attraction, and consequent repulsion, that his youthful beauty and unsophisticated good-fellowship exercise on Claggart, make it only easier for these qualities to turn envy into hatred. His very virtue makes him the target for the shaft of evil, and his quality of acceptance provokes to action its complementary opposite, the sense of frustration that can not bear the consciousness of itself, and so has to find escape in mania. Thus there develops the conflict between unconscious virtue (not even aware of its loss of Eden and unsuspecting of the presence of evil) and the bitter perversion of love which finds its only solace in destruction.

And not only Billy Budd is marked by this supreme quality of acceptance. Captain Vere, also, possesses it, but with full consciousness, and weighted with the responsibility of understanding the natural naturalness of man's volition and the unnatural naturalness of the law. In the summing up at the drum-head court-martial of the case for the law against the innocent man, he said:

> Now can we adjudge to summary and shameful death a fellow-creature innocent before God, and whom we feel to be so?—Does that state it right? You sign sad assent. Well, I too feel the full force of that. It is Nature. But do these buttons that we wear attest that our allegiance is to Nature? No, to the King. Though the ocean, which is inviolate Nature primeval, though this be the element where we move and have our being as sailors, yet as the King's officers lies our duty in a sphere correspondingly natural? . . . We fight at command. If our judgements approve the war, that is but coincidence. So in other particulars. So now, would it be not so much ourselves that would condemn as it would be martial law operating through us? For that law and the rigour of it, we are not responsible. Our vowed responsibility is in this: That however pitilessly that law may operate, we nevertheless adhere to it and administer it.

In Captain Vere we find a figure which may interestingly be compared to Pontius Pilate. Like Pilate, he condemns the just man to a shameful death, knowing him to be innocent, but, unlike Pilate, he does not wash his hands, but manfully assumes the full responsibility, and in such a way as to take the half, if not more than the half, of the bitterness of the execution upon himself. We are given to suppose that there is an affinity, a spiritual understanding between Captain Vere and Billy Budd, and it is even suggested that in their partial and separate existences they contribute two essential portions of that larger spirit which is man. Such passages as that quoted lie on the surface of this story, but they indicate the depths beneath. There are darker hints: those deep, far-away things in Vere, those occasional flashings-forth of intuition—short, quick probings to the very axis of reality. Though the book be read many times, the student may still remain baffled by Melville's significant arrangement of images. The story is so solidly filled out as to suggest dimensions in all directions. As soon as the mind fastens upon one subject, others flash into being.

Melville reported in *Pierre* how he fished his line into the deep sea of childhood, and there, as surely as any modern psychoanalyst, discovered all the major complexes that have since received baptism at the hands of Freudians. He peered as deep as any into the origins of sensuality, and in conscious understanding he was the equal of any modern psychologist; in poetic divination he has the advantage of most. No doubt the stresses of his own inner life demanded this exceptional awareness. In this book of his old age, the images which he chose for the presentation of his final wisdom, move between the antinomies of love and hate, of innocence and malice. From behind—from far behind the main pageant of the story—there seem to fall suggestive shadows of primal, sexual simplicities. In so conscious a symbolist as Melville, it would be surprising if there should be no meaning or half-meaning in the spilling of Billy's soup towards the homosexually-disposed Claggart, in the impotence of Billy's speech in the presence of his accuser, in his swift and deadly answer, or the likening of Claggart's limp, dead body to that of a snake.

It is possible that such incidents might be taken as indications of some unresolved problem in the writer himself. This may be, but when we remember how far Melville had got in the process of self-analysis in *Pierre,* and when we have glanced at the further analysis that is obvious in the long narrative poem *Clarel,* it seems likely that this final book, written nearly forty years after *Pierre,* should contain a further, deeper wisdom. And as the philosophy in it has grown from that of rebellion to that of acceptance, as the symbolic figures of unconscious forces have become always more concrete and objective, so we may assume that these hints are intentional, and that Melville was particularly conscious of what he was doing.

But let no one suppose that he would ever pin an image to his scale of value, as an entomologist would pin an insect to his board; there is always in his interpretation a wide spaciousness. He lifts some familiar object, holding it to his light, that it may glow and illumine some portion of what must always remain vast and unknown. For his suggestive use of words, and the special values he gives them, and the large implication he can in this way compress into a sentence, the passage which tells how Billy Budd was hanged from the main yard-arm of the battle-ship *Indomitable* is a good example:

> Billy stood facing aft. At the penultimate moment, his words, his only ones, words wholly unobstructed in the utterance, were these—"God bless Captain Vere!" Syllables so unanticipated coming from one with the ignominious hemp about his neck—a conventional felon's benediction directed aft towards the quarters of honour; syllables, too, delivered in the clear melody of a singing bird on the point of launching from the twig, had a phenomenal effect, not unenhanced by the rare personal beauty of the young sailor, spiritualised now through late experiences so poignantly profound.
>
> Without volition, as it were, as if indeed the ship's populace were the vehicles of some vocal current-electric, with one voice, from alow and aloft, came a resonate echo—"God bless Captain Vere!" And yet at that instant Billy alone must have been in their hearts, even as he was in their eyes.
>
> At the pronounced words and the spontaneous echo that voluminously rebounded them, Captain Vere, either through stoic self-control or a sort of momentary paralysis induced by emotional shock, stood erectly rigid as a musket in the ship-armourer's rack.
>
> The hull, deliberately recovering from the periodic roll to leeward, was just regaining an even keel, when the last signal, the preconcerted dumb one, was given. At the same moment it chanced that the vapoury fleece hanging low in the east, was shot through with a soft glory as of the fleece of the Lamb of God seen in mystical vision, and simultaneously therewith, watched by the wedged mass of upturned faces, Billy ascended; and ascending, took the full rose of the dawn.
>
> In the pinioned figure, arrived at the yard-end, to the wonder of all, no motion was apparent save that created by the slow roll of the hull, in moderate weather so majestic in a great ship heavy-cannoned.

Here is Melville at his very best, at his deepest, most poetic, and therefore at his most concentrated, most conscious. Every image has its significant implication: the very roll of the heavily-cannoned ship so majestic in moderate weather—the musket in the ship-armourer's rack; and Billy's last words are the triumphant seal of his acceptance, and they are more than that, for in this supreme passage a communion between personality at its purest, most-God-given form, and character, hard-hammered from the imperfect material of life on the battleship

*Indomitable,* is here suggested, and one feels that the souls of Captain Vere and Billy are at that moment strangely one.

In this short history of the impressment and hanging of a handsome sailor-boy, are to be discovered problems almost as profound as those which puzzle us in the pages of the Gospels. *Billy Budd* is a book to be read many times, for at each reading it will light up, as do the greater experiences of life, a beyond leading always into the unknown.

# An Introduction to *Billy Budd*

## *by Eugenio Montale*

*Billy Budd, Foretopman,* is Herman Melville's last novel; it was written in 1891, a few months before the author's death, and was published posthumously. It is a tale of the sea, set on board an English man-of-war at the end of the eighteenth century, and in atmosphere, if not in plot, foreshadows the later Conrad (*e.g., The Rover*). We have grown used to recognizing Melville as a forerunner; if we name Conrad rather than many others it is on account of certain affinities in the lives and histories as well as the art of the two writers, for the author of *Moby Dick* is bound up with the origin of much of modern literature. In 1891 Melville was old and had been silent for many years: apart from a few minor works we can say that he had been silent since 1857, that is, since the period 1846–1857 (little more than ten years) to which his major works belong. In that prodigious decade, working over the memories of his long sea voyages and perilous crossings, Melville wrote, besides his great epic *Moby Dick* (known to Italians through the version of Cesare Pavese), his other most famous books. Melville's travels, then, can be seen to have taken only a few years, certainly less than Conrad's, and his long life was thereafter dedicated to his great labor as an artist to which posterity only now, and in spite of obstacles and prejudices which still arrive from America, is beginning to render the homage it deserves.

It is possible that some Americans today, glutted with European culture and suspicious of finding themselves in the intellectual minority, wish to see in Melville a rough native writer, bogged down in heavy moralism and concerned with problems which, like all else of the Emerson period, are no longer up to date. And certainly Melville, like Poe before him, is fair game for those who try to reduce poetry to pathology. But it is equally true that for an unprejudiced European reader today, one who has the necessary perspective and avoids the fads involved in keeping always up to date, the great and heroic period

---

*"An Introduction to Billy Budd" by Eugenio Montale. From* The Sewanee Review *68 (Summer 1960): 419–22.* 

of American literature is just this decade, about 1845–1855, when (after Emerson's essays and Thoreau's *Walden,* after the first efforts of the Concord writers who transplanted and recreated in New England the truths of Carlyle and the discoveries of German romantic philosophy) the figures of Poe, Hawthorne and Melville rise into prominence.

The perfection reached by Hawthorne in *The Scarlet Letter,* or the work and the influence of Poe, with his following in Europe, no longer require comment. But of the three it is probably Melville who is nearest to us today. In him that sense of darkness and damnation which the puritan Hawthorne toned down and restrained throughout an honorable literary career which was not without its compromises, rises to Biblical heights, sometimes exploding with Manichaean violence; and it is this feeling which, after winding through the more restless of his books, from *Redburn* to *Pierre,* and after spreading over the huge fresco of *Moby Dick,* finds at last its full expression in the short but perfect *Billy Budd.* From this point of view *Billy Budd,* supported and illuminated by the books which precede it, is the crowning gem of Melville's work.

Not, obviously, in the sense of pure narrative, if we can imagine as existing side with pure poetry a pure narrative in which the pressure of the content is resolved and annulled in the rhythm of the prose. This is not entirely foreign to Melville's genius, as is shown by some episodes, or I might rather say some "days" of *Moby Dick,* and by *Benito Cereno* which contains in brief Melville's *motifs,* not so much in the characters as in its atmosphere, the same atmosphere in which the lonely Crusoesque souls of Conrad's greatest novel *Victory* were later to toss. But in *Billy Budd* the rhythm never minimizes the complexity of the inspiration. In this way Melville's poetic testament is at the same time an epic and an adventure story, a Platonic dialogue, a critical essay tinged with a revolutionary spirit, and a play: a mystery play showing the supreme sacrifice, the Christian sacrifice of the Cross.

William Budd, the twenty-year-old cabin boy, the soul *naturaliter* pure and incorruptible which Melville has created in this tale, is not yet, to tell the truth, a Christian: his place, from an orthodox point of view, can only be in that limbo of pure souls to whom revelation has not been vouchsafed. His purity is based on the natural goodness of Rousseau, the immortal principles filtered by a gloomy, rigid moralism. The ship on which he is serving at the beginning of the story is none other than the *Rights of Man,* and the innocent man pays not on the cross but on the main-yard for what human justice adjudges to be his crime. But by making Billy Budd a real man in a real period of turmoil and growth, by projecting him effortlessly into a seething cultural world (European culture in the Americans of Melville's day tried not unsuccessfully to renew itself through the myth of the new world, though without renouncing its own past), and by giving him two exceptional men as antagonists, two such typical intellectuals as Claggart and Vere: by all these things Melville raised the story of *Billy Budd* not only to a moral but also to an artistic height which is but rarely reached. *Billy Budd,* to put it simply, is a great subject in the hands of a powerful poet who has concentrated into it all the phantasms, all the idols and the secrets of a whole lifetime. Certainly the story lends itself to the most daring interpretations: I need only mention one that sees the three characters as narcissistic projections of the three ages of the author. But this explanation, like the one which sees Melville in terms of neuroses and traces the work to an unconscious Oedipus complex, seems to me sterile. In *Billy Budd* the life which gives expression with equal violence to good and evil, right and wrong, tries, but without success, to solve its own mystery. It seems as if the truth is to be found in turn in the sacrificial purity of the victim, and in the austere rigor of Vere, and even (without dismissing it as conventional Mephistophelianism) in the mad and criminal magnetism of Claggart, the Master-at-arms, a fallen angel, still; and that it remains perhaps in the end with old "Board-her-in-the-smoke," the man who knows but does not speak, and who scans the horizon with sybilline words ("A cat's paw"). But it is hard to say. Because not even in this story has Melville sacrificed to a tidy ending, not even to a negative ending, what has been called by a well-known writer the *cry* of his purity.

# Final Balance: The Prose Fragments and *Billy Budd*

*by John Seelye*

*Billy Budd* is generic to Melville's other late works, the poems and fragments discussed above. Like Rip's lilac it springs out of them, quite literally, for the mysterious old Dansker was salvaged from the portrait of Daniel Orme, and it is he, the story intimates, who alone understands Claggart's behavior towards the inoffensive "Baby" Budd. The flower poems are also evoked, for Billy's name contains the budding lily of purity, and the concern of "Rip's Lilac" with man's insistence on imposing squares on nature's heedless round is the major theme of the story, here transposed into martial versus natural law. And like so much of Melville's last work, the narrative is slow-paced, ponderous, the fable weighed down with conjecture, hypothesis, qualification. Its ending, with the double deaths of Billy and his judge, Captain Vere, is still another affirmation of Mosby's motto.

Yet in some ways *Billy Budd* seems different from much of the later work, less "mysterious," even didactic. Though more complex because it is longer, its issues seem somewhat simplified, and, though the opposition of Christly Billy and Satanic Claggart is surely diagrammatic, it appears almost melodramatic in its reduction of values. Only Captain Vere seems to give the story complexity, his deliberations acting like a balance wheel in a watch, preventing a rapid, obvious resolution of the action. Without Vere, it might be said, the story would only be concerned with the mystery of Evil. With him, it becomes involved as well with the mystery of Good. It is Vere's decision, and the debatable rationale for it, which introduces the complexity of intimation, the ambiguity which is typical of Melville's planetary structures.

Still, considering Melville's earlier concern—particularly in *Clarel*—

---

*"Final Balance: The Prose Fragments and* Billy Budd.*" From* Melville: The Ironic Diagram *by John Seelye (Evanston, Ill.: Northwestern University Press, 1970), pp. 159–72.* 

with diagrammatic characters as well as structures, it may be a mistake to consider Vere the only complex creation in the narrative. The possibility of additional complexity may be derived from a comparison of *Billy Budd* and "Bartleby," for Captain Vere resembles the lawyer of that story. Confronted by the purity of innocence and the purity of malevolence, Vere ignores absolute considerations for relative ones, while yet appealing to absolute (though temporal) order. Like the lawyer, he plays a sorrowing Pilate, in whom is found a matching of both head and heart, rational action and human sympathies. Like the lawyer, the captain owes his allegiance to the temporal world, while Billy—like the scrivener—seems to have descended from other realms.

Yet Billy shares little with Bartleby save an alliterative *"B."* Where one is pallid and drawn, the other is rosy and tanned; where one is wasted and reclusive, the other is full-bodied and gregarious. Bartleby seems the personification of Death, Billy like Life itself, the vital urge incarnate. It is his very attractiveness which has drawn so many readers to the story, as the "Handsome Sailor" himself captivates so many of his companions. But "handsome is as handsome does," and Billy is a more ambiguous creation than his appearance suggests. There is in the portrait a lower layer, like the subpigmentation in Leonardo's paintings, a certain whiteness under the rose-glow of health. Something about him, for instance, recalls the Marquis de Grandvin, that "golden wine . . . in a golden chalice." Like the marquis, he possesses qualities of "the unvitiated Adam," a great "physical beauty" coupled with "moral charm." Like him also, he has a "talismanic something," a nature which "can operate upon another nature though of a temper not favourably disposed to receive its benign influence." It is this aspect of Billy, resembling as it does the transitory effects of wine, which hints at his fragile hold on life, his resemblance to the flower his name connotes.

To understand this is in some way to understand Claggart's mysterious hatred of the beautiful Billy. Like Jackson's hatred of Redburn, it is comparable to Satan's envy of Adam and Eve, the spite of the damned towards the innocent. Redburn claims that Jackson envies his youth and good looks, but fatuous ass that he is, he grasps only the obvious.

> If askance [Claggart] eyed the good looks, cheery health, and frank enjoyment of young life in Billy Budd, it was because these went along with a nature that, as Claggart magnetically felt, had in its simplicity never willed malice or experienced the reactionary bite of that serpent (p. 78).[1]

[1] [Page numbers refer to Melville's *Billy Budd* (*An Inside Narrative*) (Chicago, 1962).]

Despite his apparent inhumanity, Claggart is more intensely mortal than his genial adversary.

During the trial, Vere dismisses Claggart's malice as a "mystery of iniquity," an apparent rationalization for the sake of expediency, but the narrator also uses this phrase in connection with the master-at-arms (p. 76). The phrase recalls Mortmain, in *Clarel,* linking Claggart even more firmly to Melville's "admirable" haters, and ultimately to Ahab: "Toward the accomplishment of an aim which in wantonness of atrocity would seem to partake of the insane, he will direct a cool judgment sagacious and sound. These men are madmen, and of the most dangerous sort, for their lunacy is not continuous, but occasional, evoked by some special object" (p. 76). Claggart's regard for Billy is like Ahab's hatred for the Whale, or like the antipathy of Mortmain towards the rosy Derwent; it is like Spagnoletto's hostility towards Fra Lippo Lippi, or the fury of the one-legged misanthrope towards the bland peddler of confidence. It is "an antipathy spontaneous and profound such as is evoked in certain exceptional mortals by the mere aspect of some other mortal, however harmless he may be, . . . called forth by this very harmlessness itself" (p. 74). This is the scorn of darkness for the silly illusions of daylight, "cynic disdain, disdain of innocence—to be nothing more than innocent!" (p. 78). Though a figure of "elemental evil . . . like the scorpion for which the Creator alone is responsible," Claggart's poison is the stinging serum of truth. In *Clarel,* the gentle victim of life, Agath, shrinks away with a cry of fright from a "crabbed scorpion," an "unblest, small, evil thing," which Rolfe calls a "small epitome of devil."

> "Wert thou an ox couldst thou thus sway?
> No, disproportionate is evil
> In influence. *Evil* do I say?
> But speak not evil of the evil:
> Evil and good they braided play
> Into one cord."
>
> (IV. iv. 24–29)

A human scorpion, Claggart yearns to sting Billy with an awareness of the essential malignity of earthly life, and though his method is evil, his intentions are not entirely so.

For Billy Budd is a representative of the serenity that was, for Melville as for Swift, the "felicity of being well deceived"; like Captain Delano he is a natural innocent, a noddy whose primitive composition makes him incapable of detecting deceit. He trusts all men, accepts appearances for what they seem, and is even foolish enough to think that he can become friends with the man who hates him most. This quality of perfect innocence inspires "grim internal merriment" in the old Dansker, whose "eccentric unsentimental old sapience, primitive in its kind" as Billy's innocence, "saw or thought it saw something which in contrast to the warship's environment looked oddly incongruous in the Handsome Sailor" (p. 70). The Dansker, like Claggart, is of the party of darkness. Where the master-at-arms is a stalking cat, the Dansker is an owl, and both see things that even Captain Vere is blind to. The warship world is the world–warship, a mechanism whose imperfection is compensated by a delicate system of balances—like the lawyer's office in "Bartleby"—and in which there is no place for perfect innocence. Billy is not of this world and does not stay long in it. A heavenly Christ, he does not have a sufficient weight of earth. His antithesis, Claggart, is entirely of clay, while Captain Vere—the man in the middle—contains a balance of parts. It is he who is the mortal Christ, who takes upon himself the responsibility for his fellow men.

Again, however, Melville's diagram is a system of qualifications: as Billy's unearthliness is qualified by his mortal stammer, so Captain Vere's sense of justness is too much reliant upon the convenience of (linear) forms. And if Claggart's dark vision in some way redeems him, the redemption takes place deep in the shadow of the rose. With Billy at one extreme and Claggart at the other, the three characters seem to present a gauge of mortality, ranging from absolute good to absolute evil, but the values represented by each undergo subtle shifts as the action progresses. As in *Pierre,* the parts revolve in a synchronized movement, so that when absolute good becomes relative evil it is confronting relative good. Lacking the linear thrust of the quester, *Billy Budd* is a "round," containing a microcosmic inclusiveness and governed by a movement in which places are exchanged like "the laughing couples down a country dance." With Melville's other rounds, it results in a cipher, a "mystery of iniquity" in which Billy is the victim, Claggart the instrument, and Captain Vere—with all his Roman love of the general good—the expedient perpetrator.

Despite the formal implications of ironic balance, it would be a mistake to assume that Melville attained a "final peace" in his last novel. Although the massive materials and movements of *Moby-Dick* are missing, the constant exchange of values suggests a corresponding restlessness. The diagrammatic complexity of characterization and the parenthetical, conjectural style, with its studied distaste for open declarations, are a subtle counterpart to the great counterthrusts of characters and styles in *Moby-Dick.* And in both books the implications of form are similar, for the drastic reduction of the linear element has not altered the meaning of the dominant, all-encompassing circle. Withdrawing behind dramatic opposition and discursive indirection, Melville purposely allows the narrative "to vindicate, as it may, its own credibility" (p. 77). But the method of *Moby-Dick* is similar, despite differences of style, and as early as *White-Jacket,* Melville allowed "Truth to vindicate itself." If Melville abandoned the heroic pose as quixotic, he never seems to have had much faith in it. He has moved his encounter from the operatic backdrop of a whale hunt to the subdued murmur of a courtroom, but his characters are as afloat as ever, drifting in a sea of conjectures.

Though not a quester, in the sense that he *knows* what he is after, Captain Vere resembles Captain Ahab in being an advocate of the linear view. As Ahab puts his faith in charts, so Vere believes that "With mankind . . . forms, measured forms, are everything; and that is the import couched in the story of Orpheus with his lyre spellbinding the wild denizens of the wood" (p. 128). Ahab overlooks the element of chance, and Vere, in considering the effect of forms on mankind, neglects to remember that the "wild denizens" tore Orpheus apart in a frenzy. Captain Vere's forms are political, "applied to the disruption of forms going on across the Channel and the consequences thereof," and his reliance upon them reflects the same fears of revolution that appear in Melville's work as early as *Mardi.* Though political forms are ultimately illusory, in that they bely the eternal flux of life, they are the only bulwark civilized man has against the chaos that is the opposite extreme. The danger is that form will become formalism—a strict advocacy of "right"—and will attempt to halt the natural, pendulumlike movement by which nature manifests its own balance, to impose a dead balance contrary to that cyclical sway. It is Captain Vere's misfortune that he is called upon by his "time and fate" to effect just such a balance. His execution of Billy, though perfectly just, is perfectly unnatural.

This seems to be the implication of the stateroom in which the trial takes place, a compartment which resembles the lawyer's office in "Bartleby," divided as it is into opposing portholes with a skylight overhead, and at the far end opposed staterooms containing the imprisoned Billy and dead Claggart. The cabin itself is described as "a goodly oblong of length coinciding with the ship's beam" (p. 105), and the word "beam," along with the perfect balance of the arrangements within, suggests the scales of justice. Billy is on one end of the "beam," Claggart on the other. The mechanism is given further complexity by the placing of the court, for Captain Vere, though "sinking his rank" in order to appear as a witness, nonetheless maintains his privileged position on the "weather side" of the "beam," which elevates him above the members of the court, who are seated on the lee side. On the literal level, Vere's position indicates his superior rank, but on the metaphorical level, it signifies the "light" weight of his minority opinion. The balance is decidedly against him, a balance represented both by the opinions of the court—who "naturally" side with Billy—and the pitch of the ship as it contends (like Vere) with natural forces.

Something further of this intimation is hinted by Vere's act of pacing, "in the returning ascent to windward climbing the slant deck in the ship's lee roll, without knowing it symbolizing thus in his action a mind resolute to surmount difficulties even if against primitive instincts strong as the wind and the sea" (p. 109). In walking up the rising deck, Vere's action is symbolic of his attempt to impose balance on the pivoting heave of nature's rhythm, and by returning to windward each time against the lee roll he is walking up the steepest incline possible—bucking both wind and tide. Like Ahab, he is imposing his will on nature, and he will suffer Ahab's fate.

We are never told in which of the opposing staterooms Billy and Claggart are placed. Their opposition is important only in regard to the matter confronting Vere and his court: "In the light of that martial code whereby it was formerly to be judged, innocence and guilt personified in Claggart and Budd in effect changed places" (p. 103). Vere is neither for nor against Billy; he is for the dead balance of martial order, the preservation of forms against the threat of flux. Like his fellow members of the court, who wish to free Billy because of his essential innocence, Vere feels the "full force of . . . Nature," but his allegiance is not to nature, it is to the king—to temporal law. Vere defines his position as "unnatural," in opposition to the instinctive feelings which would in a natural situation have acquitted Billy. Billy is "naturally" good as Claggart is "naturally" evil, but Vere stresses the irrelevance of natural ethics: "Budd's intent or non-intent is nothing to the purpose. . . . War looks but to the frontage, the appearance" (p. 112).

Billy, too, has depended on appearances, and his faith in them eventually leads to his death. Though war "looks but to the frontage," it becomes the final reality of Billy's situation, as he lies in chains "between . . . two guns, as nipped in the vice of fate." The guns are black, a "funereal hue" which contrasts with Billy's white clothing, compared to "a patch of discolored snow in early April lingering at some upland cave's black mouth" (pp. 118–19). The sullied snow is at once an image of Billy's mortality and his natural purity, a token of the unadulterated primitiveness which has been somewhat tarnished by "virgin experience of the diabolical incarnate and effective in some men." Like Adam, Billy is doomed by his encounter with the knowledge of evil, and his rosy flesh is evaporating like the snow to which he is compared: "The skeleton in the cheekbone at the point of its angle was just beginning delicately to be defined under the warm-tinted skin" (p. 119).

In contrast to Billy's fragile, natural beauty is the massiveness of the machinery around him, illuminated by the "dirty yellow light" of oil supplied by those who gain profit from "the harvest of death." The "flickering splashes" of artificial light "pollute the pale moonshine all but ineffectually struggling in obstructed flecks through the open ports from which the tampioned cannon protrude" (p. 119), much like the grass that struggles for a hold in the pavement of Bartleby's prison. Above decks, the moon (regulator of "time and tides") is bright and full, its light silvering everything "not blotted by the clear-cut shadows horizontally thrown of fixtures and moving men" (p. 116). Here, as below, man and his objects are linear and fixed, "polluting" and "blotting" the pure light of nature. Even the sailors for whom Billy is to become a sort of Christ govern themselves by "strict adherence to usage," part of the mechanism upon which he is crucified. In their simple way they are given to "forms" as much as their captain.

The third emblematic juxtaposition of law and nature, of fixed forms and fluid rhythm, occurs during Billy's execution: singing his final benediction, the "Handsome Sailor" rises birdlike into the air, his departure timed to coincide with the arrival of the ship at "an even keel," his death a witness of Vere's maintenance of dead balance. "In the pinioned figure arrived at the yard-end, to the wonder of all no motion was apparent, none save that created by the slow roll of the hull in moderate weather, so majestic in a great ship ponderously cannoned" (p. 124). But Billy does not "die." We are never told specifically that he is a man being hung—he "ascends"—and we are not told that he is dead. Indeed, he is still in motion, like a pendulum swinging in time to the roll of the ponderous warship, its "majesty" caught in the pulsating rhythm of nature. The moment of dead balance has been only a moment, and the rhythm continues its rise and fall. The victim is not Billy Budd—it is Captain Vere. Where he is blessed by Billy he becomes "rigid as a musket," paralyzed by the "shock" of innocent irony. All his motions are those of a man who has been hung, while Billy, birdlike, ascends.

The reaction of the crew to Billy's death, at first a dumb silence, then "a sound not easily to be verbally rendered," introduces the fourth juxtaposition of law and nature. This sound, the crew's instinctive reaction to the sight they have just witnessed, is the threatening release of emotions which is a sign of man's primitiveness, and it is compared to the "sloping advance through precipitous woods" of "the freshet-wave of a torrent suddenly swelled by pouring showers in tropical mountains." The narrator ironically passes off the "muffled murmur" as "inarticulate," and therefore "dubious in significance further than it seemed to indicate some capricious revulsion of thought or feeling such as mobs ashore are liable to, in the present instance possibly implying a sullen revocation on the men's part of their involuntary echoing of Billy's benediction."

But the narrator's demurrer is weakened by Melville's customary qualifications, the "possibly" and "seemed," and the facetious context of "inarticulate," "sullen," and "capricious." The murmur is sympathetic, like the feelings of the court a natural response, and it is countered by the strategically timed piping of the new watch. Unlikely music, the "silver whistles of the boatswain and his mates" have the Orphic effect of piercing "that ominous low sound [and] dissipating it." The irony is that the music is scarcely the soothing strain that one associates with Orpheus. It is harsh, discordant, "unnatural"—like the system it enforces.

A second and more ominous murmur attends Billy's burial, when the sailors are aroused by the circling of sea birds over the burial spot. But this superstitious reaction (keyed by nature) is not tolerated and is quelled by the drum beat to quarters, "which familiar sound happening at least twice every day, had upon the present occasion a signal peremptoriness in it. True martial discipline long continued superinduces in average man a sort of impulse whose operation at the official word of command much resembles in its promptitude the effect of an instinct" (p. 127). The response, again, is achieved by "music"—forms—but the "instincts" so affected are not natural. They are "a sort of" impulse which "much resembles" instinct but which has been "superinduced"—imposed on man's natural independence.

The consequences and the tenuous sway of such an imposition is suggested by the background of mutiny and revolution against which the narrative is enacted. Vere, the fool of forms, is eventually killed by a bullet fired by a soldier of the French Republic "from a porthole of the enemy's main cabin," the windward counterpart of the porthole from which he stared during Billy's trial. Eventually his advocacy of temporal order is belied by the overruling laws of nature, and the captain dies with Billy's name on his lips. But for a time the forces of form win out, and Billy's death is followed by a re-establishment of order and routine, though with a slight variation, as if somewhat out of focus.

> At this unwonted muster at quarters, all proceeded as at the regular hour. The band on the quarter-deck played a sacred air, after which the chaplain went through the customary morning service. That done, the drum beat the retreat; and toned by music and religious rites subserving the discipline and purposes of war, the men in their wonted orderly manner dispersed to the places allotted them when not at the guns.
>
> And now it was full day. The fleece of low-hanging vapor had vanished,

> licked up by the sun that late had so glorified it. And the circumambient air in the clearness of its serenity was like smooth white marble in the polished block not yet removed from the marble-dealer's yard.
>
> (p. 128)

These two paragraphs are like a seal upon the ambiguity of the story, for above the formal, ordered activities of man, nature maintains its own order, the cyclical progress of the sun. Rising, the sun disperses the rosy clouds that gave Billy's ascent a seemingly mystical importance, as death has dissipated the rosy healthfulness of the sailor himself. All appearance is a trick of light. A perfect blank remains, "circumambient air" as white and serene as a block of marble hewn from a quarry—an image which contains at once a circle and a square, tokens of nature's round completeness and man's imposition of linear symmetry upon it.

This image, like the unfinished, imperfect narrative which contains it, is a final seal to Melville's many ambiguities. As blank as the Whale, the block of marble is serenely mysterious, latent with or perhaps innocent of particular meaning. Like the new tabernacle in "Rip Van Winkle's Lilac," it is testimony to man's persistence in squaring nature's circle, but the circle cannot be squared, and the block—like all fiction—is artifice, is a lie. Moreover, it is as yet incomplete and awaits the definition of an artist's chisel—some relievo or legend—or perhaps reshaping into an imitation of a natural form. Still, as it stands, the marble block most resembles a tombstone, a further hint that only death can provide the symmetry of pure fiction, can solve the final mystery, and it is with the death song of Billy that the story ends, as the chains that bound him to life and law dissolve into the oozy weeds fathoms down.

# The White Hue of Nothingness

*by Paul Brodtkorb, Jr.*

Is Vere, then, "right" or "wrong"? Society's measured forms are all that exist; they are empty of ethical content because individual, human, measured forms (the judicious moral estimates we make of others, the discrete characters of others as we read them) have no content in *time* beyond spontaneous energy finding unpredictable expression. This condition need not demand that Vere should not have judged Billy: to be able to act at all in such circumstances requires judgment, and society requires that we act, therefore that we judge. But Vere may well be wrong in his *particular* judgment; this, however, we as critics can argue over eternally; for the story is not clear on the specific implications of alternative judgments, providing, as it does, merely the "boggy ground" of various might-have-beens [*Billy Budd* (*An Inside Narrative*) (Chicago, 1962), p. 57] to build conclusions on. Insulated as Vere's language and reading show his temperament to be, insulated as that temperament must therefore finally be from what is going on in the unread, unintelligent (but feeling, and possibly plotting) minds of the lower ranks, Vere has no way of knowing the outcome of various alternative judgments. Nor in fact do we. Because neither he nor we can predict the further acts of the muttering sailors, we cannot escape subjectivity: both he and we must choose in darkness, then rationalize our choice. And neither he nor we can coerce by force of personality the acceptance of our best choices, as Nelson, or Ahab, could: the old heroes are gone with the old ships. *Any* particular pragmatic choice must therefore be wrong in that better possibilities will soon rankle in the mind to sour it; and the only "right" choice, the ideal one of clemency for Billy, would, so far as Vere or we can know, become *fully* right solely by the accident of enough of the elements potentially there for once coming together in harmony, but to make this morally more adequate choice would be to leave everything in the lap of the absent, or inattentive, gods. Vere's choice "says" man cannot escape responsi-

---

bility for his acts even when he is not responsible; beyond that, it might very well be wrong.

I would say, then, that *Billy Budd* implies that virtue and vice are relative even when they seem, as at first they do in Billy and Claggart, nearly absolute. They are relative because they reveal themselves to us only in the fluid dimensions of time, not the static eternity suitable to such moral abstractions; they reveal themselves in the accidental circumstances of historical context, in the temporal events that bring virtue and vice into problematic collision. As Pierre once said to Isabel: "Look: a nothing is the substance, it casts one shadow one way, and another the other way; and these two shadows cast from one nothing—these, it seems to me, are Virtue and Vice." [1] Or, as in the ballad Billy asks, "But aren't it all sham?" I would argue that the story escapes advocating either conservative or liberal moral choices, eludes liberal or conservative critical rhetoric, and retreats onto a twilit ground where few important human actions are rationally choosable.

If it does, then about Vere's particular choice, as about Vere's (and perhaps society's) ultimate sanity, "every one must determine for himself" in the very dubious light the narrative affords; and "who in the rainbow" *can* "draw the line where the violet tint ends and the orange tint begins?" (p. 102). The plain fact is that no one can, for what the story provides is mystery that is almost but not quite solvable. The moral forms we impose on it do not, in the end, fit well; which may help to explain why, despite all the story's Christian imagery and allusiveness, the archetype of the crucifixion applies only unsatisfactorily and up to a point; and to explain, also, why Billy, though of heroic physical mold and admired by many of his fellow seamen and evoking from the narrator comparison with so many legendary heroes, is finally "not presented as a conventional hero" (p. 53); and why art's "symmetry of form" is incompatible with the "ragged edges" of "truth uncompromisingly told" (p. 128). *Billy Budd* is architecturally unfinished because it explicitly tries to deal with "fact" (p. 128), but, as Vere, for one, knows, while artistic conventions will neatly organize the world of facts, they do so in human temporality only by simplifying and, therefore, by falsifying our full sense of that world. *Being,* here, no less than in *Moby-Dick,* is tinged with the white hue of nothingness. Because it is, interpretational warfare has followed. The story impresses us as an allegorical fable of some sort, and fables have often to do with moral events to which we can respond with some moral precision. To help us so respond, we have, as critics, given the story clearly measured forms, Aristotelian or Christian or Freudian or

[1] *Pierre* (New York, 1949), Bk. 19, II, p. 322.

Jungian; we have, like the narrator, invoked authorities and clarified terms. Because, like the narrator, and even like his characters, we prefer definable moral issues, and justified action, and judicial murder, and war, to suspension of what we think we fundamentally believe about the world: in belief resides identity.

Therefore we stake ourselves on what we see in books, just as on what we see in life. This book, more than most, invites our either/or interpretational response: it presents us with basic enigmas, begins to structure them in alternative moral terms, then, in part because that is the way we habitually understand things, asks us to choose; and, in this era of Adolf Eichmann and Viet Nam when so much depends upon our taking stands, passionately, so we do. If the inevitable outcome of measured forms is like murder, that of finally unmeasurable forms like *Billy Budd* is like life, if art is like life or can generate it.[2]

More than thirty years ago Grant Watson,[3] responding perhaps to the story's apparent serenity of tone, called *Billy Budd* a "testament of acceptance." That formulaic phrase probably invites identification of Billy with the elderly Melville; Lewis Mumford, Watson's predecessor in this kind of reading, had put it like this: "As Melville's own end approached, he cried out with Billy Budd: God bless Captain Vere! In this final affirmation Hermann Melville died." [4]

One would think that Billy is rather too ignorant in his innocence to embody Melville's experience; but his innocence may yet lead to something that in the end Melville aspired to—something, of course, that the whole story must serve as a context for and qualify. Billy faces his own death, the ultimate and radically personal nonbeing, and, whether or not "willing" it, he faces it with a mysterious serenity. Brought to his present confrontation with death by his prior inability to speak and thereby to formulate the complex into the simple, facing this final enigma which is the essence of all mystery, Billy is silent once more. As far as the story presents him, he is silent in his cell: we never hear his words; in a curious way, Billy is silent even on the scaffold, where his "God bless Captain Vere" is "a conventional felon's benediction" (p. 123) "so unanticipated coming from" Billy that as a speech his words are a perfect enigma, as his whole manner of death

[2] If my contention in the early pages of this essay [in its original form] is right (that Melville's manuscript contains an *Ur-Billy-Budd* plus incompatible descendants, and that each critic addresses one or another discrete Billy, tending to omit, because unaware of, shadow Billies that stand behind the one he sees) then perhaps, to take only two of the many good published interpretations, a reading such as Milton Stern's in *The Fine Hammered Steel of Herman Melville* (Urbana, Ill., 1957) is addressed more to what Melville had in mind at the outset.

[3] "Melville's Testament of Acceptance," *NEQ*, VI (June 1933), 319–327. [Reprinted in this volume, p. 11.]

[4] *Herman Melville* (New York, 1929), p. 357.

increasingly becomes an enigma; then, he is suddenly "gone, and in a measure mysteriously gone" (p. 131). In short, nearing the end, Billy, so close to nature now and like it a moral enigma, ceases to speak to us, and ceases to act, as if in the face of his life and his death acting and speech were pointless or unnecessary or impossible.

Walter Sutton[5] has used Melville's poem "Buddha" from the *Timoleon* volume of 1891 to gloss what he thinks Melville's attitude was:

> Swooning swim to less and less,
> Aspirant to nothingness!
> Sobs of the worlds, and dole of kinds
> That dumb endurers be—
> Nirvana! absorb us in your skies,
> Annul us into thee.

Between 1888 and 1891, reading and carefully annotating seven volumes of Schopenhauer at the end of a life that had known many ways of annihilation, from the loss of literary fame to the abrupt, senseless deaths of his two sons, Melville may well have wished to be able, like the pagan Billy, to accept: not eternal Christian salvation, not even the temporal ways of man, but nothingness: the nothingness within humanity of *The Confidence Man,* the nothingness which is the ground of all being in *Moby-Dick,* the nothingness fast coming out of his own future to meet him as he wrote and constantly, ambiguously revised this final story that provides such a rich harvest for all of us "entomological" critics.

And, plainly, part of that harvest is there simply because Melville spent too long on *Billy Budd.* Even *Moby-Dick* was the result of a sustained and relatively short burst of effort, so that, despite all its seeming vagaries, it is the product of a unified consciousness; while *Billy Budd,* which even after his five years of work on it was regarded by Melville's wife as unfinished, seems to chronicle a divided consciousness; divided not by irony alone but by the reading and reflection and changing thoughts and attitudes of those five years of revisions and reconceptions. In my interpretation of the story, it is, in fact, Melville's inability to finish it that eventually and perhaps inevitably became his narrative's subject matter.

Possibly, though, if there is any sort of a "final" attitude in the story it is to be found in a viewpoint that from time to time breaks through over the shoulder of its narrator, a viewpoint that, though always focussed on humanity in *this* world, is secretly located in the void of eternity far from the false perspectives and lexicons of history

[5] "Melville and the Great God Budd," *Prairie Schooner,* XXXIV (Summer 1960), 128–133.

and historians and even poets. What the story watches is the wrangles of men, at once so momentous and so petty, made up as they are of death and spilled soup. But what the story silently records is Melville's last and dogged making up of his mind (as he once prematurely told Hawthorne that he had "pretty much" done[6]) to be annihilated. If this is the story's inmost "inside narrative," it explains why one's over-all impression of *Billy Budd* is of something like patience, directed at passion. The serenity of Melville's "acceptance," it seems to me, is real enough as *serenity;* though it is not like the serenity of Nirvana or Christian resignation, but more like that of an infinite and in the end gentle despair accepted by a man about to leave the merely human world of time.

[6] See Hawthorne's journal entry for Nov. 1856, quoted in Jay Leyda, *The Melville Log* (New York, 1951), II, 529.

# The Ceremony of Innocence

## *by William York Tindall*

*Billy Budd* seems to make something almost too tidy out of what remains uncertain in *Moby Dick.* Melville's story of the captain, the villain, and the tar, apparently less a story than a commentary on one, may strike the hasty reader as a product of reason rather than imagination, as something reduced to discourse for ready apprehension by basic Englishmen. What had to be said has been said by Captain Vere or Melville himself. As critics, therefore, we may feel frustrated, as Romantics we may prefer a little teasing mystery around, and as esthetes, confronted with discourse, we are sure that talking about a thing is less admirable than embodying it in image or action. Of Kierkegaard's three categories, the esthetic, the moral, and the divine, Melville seems to have chosen the second—to the applause of some and the departure of others, for *Don Giovanni* maybe.

That the matter of *Billy Budd* gratifies what Melville calls "the moral palate" is plain from the plainest rehearsal. The scene is a British frigate during the Napoleonic wars. Two mutinies have justified fears of more. Against this ominous background, Billy, an innocent aboard, is accused for no good reason by Claggart, a petty officer, of plotting mutiny. The captain, a reasonable man, doubts Claggart's story and brings Billy in to confront his lying accuser. Overcome by a stutterer's indignation, the innocent foretopman, unable to speak a word, strikes Claggart dead with a fist like a ham. Captain Vere is faced with a dilemma. Though he believes in Billy's innocence, naval law and prudence alike demand punishment for the impetuous seaman while pity and reason counsel mercy. Internal debate inclines the captain toward conviction, and Billy, condemned despite the "troubled conscience" of his judges, is hanged.

The subject is a quandary or what Melville calls "the intricacies involved in the question of moral responsibility." As the captain ponders "the moral phenomenon presented in Billy Budd" and the

---

*"The Ceremony of Innocence" by William York Tindall. From* Great Moral Dilemmas in Literature, Past and Present, *edited by R. M. MacIver (New York: Harper & Row, Publishers, Inc., 1956), pp. 73–81.* 

"elemental evil" of Claggart, he fathoms the "mystery of iniquity." The case of Billy seems, as the captain says, a matter for "psychologic theologians."

Although, as T. S. Eliot observes in *After Strange Gods,* "It is . . . during moments of moral and spiritual struggle . . . that men [in fiction] . . . come nearest being real," Billy and Claggart, who represent almost pure good and pure evil, are too simple and too extreme to satisfy the demands of realism; for character demands admixture. Their all but allegorical blackness and whiteness, however, are functional in the service of Vere's problem, and Vere, goodness knows, is real enough. Claggart is black because, as Philipp G. Frank once observed, a sinner is necessary for the realization of a moral code; and an innocent is almost equally instructive. These abstractions, a sacrifice of verisimilitude to tactical necessity, reveal the "moral quality" of the captain's mind, which becomes a theater for contending opposites and eventual choice. Such dramatic crises are not only the favorite stuff of novelists but of philosophers and poets as well: Kierkegaard wrote *Either/Or* and Yeats "The Choice."

Not only rational, Vere's choice involves his whole sensitive, adult being. Agony shows on his face as he emerges from his interview with Billy, and a final exclamation shows how deeply he is stirred. Involving more than black and white, the captain's choice is between two moral codes, military and natural. The first is evident; the second is either that of the noble savage, in whom Melville was interested, or what Western culture takes for granted. In other words, the captain's conflict is between the balanced claims of justice and equity, order and confusion, law and grace, reason and feeling, or, as Melville puts it, "military duty" and "moral scruple." Vere's eloquent and moving speech to the drumhead court, the climax of such drama as there is, leaves little to add about these issues and his dilemma.

The conflict of military with natural may occupy the stage, but Melville recognizes other codes, that of custom or respectability, for example. Claggart's "natural depravity" appears in respectable guise. Melville also recognizes the cultural, psychological, and absolute bases for morality, and hints in a very modern way at their operation.

"Moral," Melville's favorite word—in this book at least—is one which, though commonly taken for granted, is slippery. I have read a thing in which "moral" means something else on every page. What Yvor Winters means by it escapes me. Vague and general like F. R. Leavis's "awareness of life" or narrow and definite like the *quid agas* of Scholastic philosophers, the word needs fixing before use. As I shall use it and as I think Melville did, morality implies not only action but motive, attitude, and being. It involves a sense of obligation to self, community, and the absolute, which provide a frame by conscience, law, tradition, or revelation. If we demand a single equivalent, Melville's "responsibility" will do.

Vere's action, however sudden and whether we approve of it or not, is plainly responsible. Billy and Claggart act, to be sure: one bears false witness and the other delivers a blow, but neither actor follows reason and each is more important for what he is than what he does. If being as well as action can be moral, however, they are moral figures, too, existing like cherubs or fiends in a moral atmosphere. Good and bad, they occupy the region of good and evil.

It is agreed by most that moral substance is necessary for the novel. Not the pure form of Flaubert's desire, and falling far short of the condition of music, the novel is an arrangement of references to vital issues, without which it is empty. A value of Joyce's *Ulysses,* for example, is the feeling and idea of charity. That moral substance fails to insure greatness, however, is proved by the works of Horatio Alger; and that it fails to guarantee moral effect is proved by those of Mickey Spillane. The errors of censors and formalists show the folly of judging by morality alone or arrangement alone. Not moral idea but its embodiment in what Eliot called objective correlatives, suitably arranged, determines value. Far from inciting action as moralizing does, embodied morality invites contemplation, and to become an object of contemplation, substance must be distanced by form. The question is not how much morality is there but how much is under control, how fully insight and moral intelligence have submitted to esthetic discipline. Our problem, then, is not morality itself but moral art or morally significant form.

Captain Vere's speech to the court adequately embodies the idea of "moral responsibility" in dramatic form; but we must find if Billy's history has found fitting embodiment. At first reading, that history seems a curious and eccentric structure of essays on ethics, digressions or "bypaths," character sketches, and chronicles of the navy, an arrangement that after uncertain progress tails inconclusively off. Such image and action as we find, failing to halt the lamentable decline, seem occasions for analysis or digression, like biblical texts in a pulpit. Since the crucial interview between Vere and Billy is disappointingly offstage, Melville seems to have avoided the dramatic possibilities of his theme. That the book calls for the dramatization he failed to give it, is proved by attempts at play and opera, which, while affirming excellence of theme, imply that action or image are better ways of presenting it. But something that continues to fascinate us in its present form and calls forth responses beyond the capacity of discourse, suggests art of another kind. Maybe Melville avoided drama in the interests of a less obvious medium.

*Moby Dick* assures us that Melville was an artist, not a lecturer on ethics. He not only worked three years on *Billy Budd,* but he seems to have regarded the result with far from senile favor. The first version, recently detected in manuscript by F. Barron Freeman, reveals more action and less discourse; yet this version, which corresponds more happily to what we think fiction should be, is not so effective as the one before us with all its weight of digression and analysis.

That Melville was aware of form is clear from passages in *Billy Budd.* When Captain Vere says, "With mankind forms, measured forms, are everything," he probably means usage and custom; but Melville himself, applying Vere's remark to esthetics, says that the symmetry of form desirable in pure fiction cannot be achieved in factual narrative like this. The story is not factual in fact. But Melville, wanting it to seem so, excuses apparent formlessness as a form for giving the illusion of a bare report; for truth, he continues, will always have its ragged edges and matters of fact must lack the finish of an "architectural finial." Aware of loose structure and inconclusive ending, he justifies them for what seem wrong reasons. Not reasons, however, but what he made must detain us while we scout further possibilities. The curious form he made may be functional and, for all our hasty impression and his explanation, effective. Is the book as shapeless as he implies? Or, if shapeless, is shapelessness a kind of shape? Is the book as pedestrian, discursive, and factual as he claims and as we had supposed on first looking into it?

What seems at first to be factual is presented, we find, in part by images and allusions that are incompatible with a pretense of factuality. Though unapparent, those images are livelier than we thought. Consider the coloring of the scene between decks before the execution as Billy lies in white amid profound blackness. Catching up the abstract whiteness and blackness of Billy and Claggart, this image of black and white embodies them. At the execution the rosy dawn that seems "the fleece of the Lamb of God seen in mystical vision" promises a kind of renewal while implying much else. Circling birds after the burial at sea offer by the aid of tradition some spiritual import. And that spilt soup, perhaps more action than image, carries suggestions beyond the demands of plot, suggestions so indefinite, what is more, that they confound its rational progress. Even the names of ships, though serving a more comprehensible purpose, are as significant as those in *Moby Dick.* Billy is removed from the *Rights of Man,* for instance, and Vere is mortally wounded by a shot from the *Athéiste.*

The words of *Billy Budd* carry more than denotation. "Sinister dexterity," at once witty and desolating, sounds like something from *Finnegans Wake,* where, indeed, it reappears. Vere's last words, "Billy Budd," are equivocal. Do they imply feeling, regret, self-realization, understanding? Are they a form for something incompletely realized?

However "factual" the words of this pseudoreport, they function like the words of poetry.

Not only last words and indeterminate images but a number of hints about Billy's "all but feminine" nature plague our assumptions. Roses and lilies dye his cheeks. He comports himself like a "rustic beauty" at times and like a vestal virgin at others. These qualities and appearances, astonishing in an able seaman, calling forth an "ambiguous smile" from one or another of his shipmates, suggest psychological depths and motives below the level of the plain report. By virtue of such intimations Billy seems at once more and less bottomless than we had supposed, and so do the motives of Claggart, if not those of the captain himself. Among such suggestions, avoidance of the obviously dramatic becomes implicit embodiment that escapes the limits of drama.

What pleases me most, however, is the accompaniment of biblical allusions which, however unobtrusive and irregular, recur like Wagnerian *leitmotiv*. Time and again Billy is compared to Adam and Jesus. Billy's innocence is as much that of Adam before the Fall as that of the more secular noble savage. As a "peacemaker," a term implying beatitude, Billy seems destined for "crucifixion"; and his hanging, condensing events, becomes an ascension. Vere is compared to Abraham about to sacrifice Isaac, obeying God's will with fear and trembling. Becoming a shadow of God, Vere weighs the claims of Adam and Satan. Claggart, whose denunciation is reported in Mosaic terms as "false witness," is compared not only to the Serpent of Eden but to Ananias and to one struck dead by an angel of God, "yet," as the captain says, "the angel must hang!" Man's fall and redemption and all troubles between seem suggested by this large though not fully elaborated analogy, which, bringing to mind the mythical parallels in *Ulysses* and *The Waste Land,* removes Billy a little farther from the abstraction to which, for all his stutter and those rosy cheeks, he seems committed. However incapable of supporting this mythical burden, he becomes by its aid almost as portentous as choosing Vere. The sailors, whose testimony cannot be ignored, are more impressed by Billy than by Vere, reason and all. Not only being and secular victim, Billy becomes saint and martyr and his hanging an omen. Pieces of the spar to which he quietly ascends are venerated like pieces of the true cross, suitable for reliquaries or the holiest of duffle bags. By the aid of myth and military ritual the story of Billy, transformed from an essay on good, evil, and choice, approaches what Yeats called "the ceremony of innocence."

We must conclude that Melville avoided the attractions of the obvious in the interests of indefinite suggestiveness and myth. His work, whatever its air of the factual and the discursive, is symbolist and richer for scarcity of drama and image. Such drama and images as are there function more intensely in their abstract context than profusion could. That the structure as a whole also serves esthetic purpose is likely. As we have seen, the book is a queer arrangement of discourse, action, image, and allusion, with discourse predominating. We have seen how image and action work in this mixture; but we must examine the function of discourse. In such context, discourse, increasing tension, makes allusion and image dramatic or enlarges them, and, working with allusion, image, and action may produce a third something by juxtaposition as in Eliot's *Four Quartets* or Wallace Stevens' *Notes Toward a Supreme Fiction*. Seeming now a structure of conflicts, not only of men and codes but of methods, which become a technical echo of the theme, the book emerges as a structural drama or a drama of structure. An ending that seemed weak afterthought (and was not there in the first version) now unifies all. Vere's exclamation, the saint's legend, and inconclusiveness, working together, comprise a form, which may tail off but tails suggestively off, leaving endless reverberations in our minds. There is more mystery around than we had thought, and we may agree with dying Gertrude Stein that answers are less important than questions. What at a superficial reading had the appearance of exhaustive discourse becomes inexhaustible. The shapeless thing becomes suggestive shape. Neither as loose nor as tight as it once seemed, the strange sequence of precise discourse and indefinite suggestiveness corresponds to our experience of life itself. That the form Melville made fascinates while it eludes and teases is shown no less by popular favor than by the abundance of critical comment.

However different it looks, *Billy Budd* is not altogether different in kind from *Moby Dick,* another structure of digression, discourse, action, and image. The proportions and impact may be different, the images of *Moby Dick* may be more compelling, but both serve symbolic suggestion and both are forms for offering a vision of reality. Not the tidy discourse of our first impression, the work is almost as inexplicable as *Moby Dick*.

What exactly does this form present? It is impossible to answer this question for any symbolist work; for works of this kind escape discursive accounting. We may say that *Billy Budd* is a vision of man in society, a vision of man's moral quandary or his responsibility; but its meaning is more general than these, and that is why it haunts us. So haunted, I find the work not an essay on a moral issue but a form for embodying the feeling and idea of thinking about a moral issue, the experience of facing, of choosing, of being uneasy about one's choice, of trying to know. Not a conclusion like a sermon, *Billy Budd* is a vision of confronting what confronts us, of man thinking things out with all the attendant confusions and uncertainties. Disorder is a form for this and the apparently formless book a formal triumph. To do what it does it has to be a fusion of tight–loose, shapeless–shaped, irrelevant–precise, suggestive–discursive—a mixture of myth, fact, and allusion that has values beyond reference. The discursive parts represent our attempts at thinking, while the action, images, and allusions represent what we cannot think but must approximate. Arrangement of these discordant elements forms a picture of a process.

From my guess at meaning it follows that the center of this form is neither Vere nor Billy but rather the teller of the story or Melville himself. Though ghostlier, he is not unlike the Marlow of Conrad's *Lord Jim* and *Heart of Darkness* or the Quentin of Faulkner's *Absalom, Absalom!* Using Vere and Billy as materials, Melville's thought-process, like those of Marlow and Quentin, is the heart of this darkness and its shape the objective correlative, a form for something at once imperfectly understood and demanding understanding. Morality, the substance of this form, becomes an element that limits and directs the feelings and ideas created by the whole. Moral substance, what is more, may be what engages our minds while the form does its work. Value, not from morality alone, issues from the form that includes it and in which it serves. If the form concerned less, I repeat it, it would be trivial, but without its formal presentation the morality would remain in Sunday school.

United now, the beautiful and the good create a vision larger than either, a vision transcending the case of Billy Budd or the quandary of Captain Vere. The teller, now any man, presents man's feeling in the face of any great dilemma. Thought and feeling, outdistancing themselves, become objects of contemplation, remote yet immediate. The effect of this form is moral in the sense of enlarging our awareness of human conditions or relationships and of improving our sensitivity In such a form Kierkegaard's esthetic, moral, and divine become a single thing.

# *Billy Budd*—Acceptance or Irony

*by Richard Harter Fogle*

There appear to be three principal conceptions of the meaning of Melville's *Billy Budd*: the first, and most heavily supported, that it is Melville's "Testament of acceptance," his valedictory and his final benediction. "There are not many final works," remarks Newton Arvin, "that have so much the air as *Billy Budd, Foretopman* has of being a Nunc Dimittis. Everyone has felt this benedictory quality about it." The second view, a reaction against the first, holds that *Billy Budd* is ironic, and that its real import is precisely the opposite of its ostensible meaning. Lawrance Thompson feels that Melville is still quarreling with God. Still a third interpretation denies that interpretation is possible; a work of art has no meaning at all that can be abstracted from it, nor is a man's work in any way an index of his character or his opinions. Thus Stanley Edgar Hyman in a lively and malicious survey of Melville scholarship denies the possibility of any certain conclusions about what manner of man Melville actually was:

> If all these basic questions about Melville, from his view of the absolute to his sexual leanings, are unanswerable, and if Melville is like Shakespeare ultimately unknowable, it is due to our inability to penetrate this mask, which is simply the mask or persona of art. Behind it the artist sits in darkness and anonymity, perhaps, as Joyce suggests, paring his nails. "Strike through the mask," Ahab exhorts us. How can we? Why in fact should we? In the last analysis it is the mask itself we want, and the face we see mirrored in it can only be our own.

All three of these views of *Billy Budd* are in their own sense true. As a highly complex work of art *Billy Budd* provides ample evidence for all. Melville certainly accepts his own imagined characters, action, and situation in good faith. Billy, Vere, and Claggart are treated with seriousness and dignity, as is the tragic complication which destroys them. On the other hand, it is also true that *Billy Budd* is pervasively ironic. Yet its irony is neither the irony of concealment nor the irony

---

*"Billy Budd—Acceptance or Irony" by Richard Harter Fogle. From* Tulane Studies in English *8 (1958): 107–13.* 

of deceit; it does not change the boldly delineated face of the story, nor its explicit and fundamental affirmations. With whatever allowances one wishes to make, Billy and Vere are still good men, Claggart is still evil, and the action is still tragic. *Billy Budd* is both ironic and ambiguous, but its ironies and ambiguities are Melville's acceptance of the limits of interpretation: they are intended neither to confuse nor to mock. His world is as always organically one and yet incomprehensible, containing the conception of an absolute truth which is yet too complex and too far away for the vision of man to encompass. There is also in *Billy Budd* the effect of an ambiguity which is not the ambiguity of art, and which needs to be taken into account. Carefully written as it no doubt was, it is not quite a finished product ready for publication. It is sometimes tentative simply for lack of a final decision which would have had to be made.

One sees how the "ironic" interpretation has arisen. It would be easy, for example, to read a devastating irony into the sequence of events immediately following Billy's execution. Step by step the crew, the natural men of the story, are diverted, misled, diffused into impotence by their officers, themselves the automatons of the mutiny act by which their world is governed. Step by step tradition and law are subtly perverted to meet the circumstances, as the starboard watch is dismissed to thin the crowd, all hands are again called together swiftly for the funeral, to be dispersed again by the drum beating to quarters. Everything is orderly but a little out of order; and the sequence of displacement follows the same pattern as Captain Vere's illegal bolstering of the law at Billy's trial. We remember that strict observation of the forms would have demanded delay until the *Indomitable* had rejoined the fleet, and Billy could be brought before the admiral. From the general point of view for the moment proposed here a single sentence could be used to epitomize the whole: "Shrill as the shriek of the sea-hawk the whistles of the Boatswain and his Mates pierced that ominous low sound, dissipating it; and yielding to the mechanism of discipline the throng was thinned by one half." The boatswains' whistles could well be the exultant scream of the bird of heaven, the sky-god's emissary, over the defeat and death of poor humanity. One recalls Tashtego and the sea-hawk at the sinking of the *Pequod.* The hawk at once exults and commands. Vere's use of form and ceremony constitutes a definite pattern.

This is not, however, the true emphasis of *Billy Budd.* To suppose it was would be to conceive an impossible perversion of values, would render Melville a crafty masochist and madman. Such an interpretation, furthermore, would have to be imported from without, and would present a distorted picture which laid inordinate stress upon Melville's rebelliousness and his reliance upon eighteenth-century rationalism. The action of Captain Vere in skilfully checking incipient revolt is based upon the settled and disinterested beliefs of a lifetime, in terms of the preparation which Melville has laid down; Vere acts for the general welfare.

> "With mankind" he would say "forms, measured forms are everything; and that is the import couched in the story of Orpheus with his lyre spell-binding the wild denizens of the woods." And this he once applied to the disruption of forms going on across the Channel and the consequences thereof.

There is perhaps a lurking irony in this Orpheus passage, but it signifies not a total reversal of its ostensible meaning but a consciousness of its incompleteness. As with all general maxims, it leaves something more to be said.

*Billy Budd* is, it seems to me, entirely comprehensible as Melville's version of tragedy. But to affirm this it is necessary to provide some definition both of tragedy and of irony as the terms are used here, though no more is attempted than an informal description sufficient for the immediate purpose. Tragedy, then, is a heightened and dignified action, intentionally so complicated as to involve its personae in the greatest conceivable difficulties, in order to elicit from them in their struggle the fullest potentialities of which they are capable. As to irony, we know that there are many notions of it, and perhaps no certain center can be found. We shall need to distinguish between different usages in order to specify the respects in which *Billy Budd* is or is not ironic. It is not ironic in the sense of irony ordinarily used by those who claim that it is; that is, a more or less complete reversal of the ostensible meaning, with, to add the words of A. R. Thompson in *The Dry Mock,* an effect of painful mockery. It is not painful, it is not sharp-edged, except by distortion of a part to misrepresent the total effect. It is ironic in that it frequently means more—not other—than it seems to say. Correspondingly *Billy Budd* is ironic in the modern sense of irony somewhat overworked by T. S. Eliot—who called it wit—, I. A. Richards, and the New Critics: that is, a consciousness of the difficulties which any belief or attitude must face, an awareness of complexity. Indeed, one might concede to *Billy Budd* any ironies, of character, word, situation, or general attitude, which do not impeach its essential good faith and render verbalization itself a worthless currency. But precisely this destructive irony is what the ironist critics have fixed upon.

*Billy Budd* can like *Moby Dick* be justly described as Melville's nineteenth-century version of classical tragedy, with old forms revivified by new issues. According to Aristotelean prescription it portrays men as better than they are. The principals are exceptional: Billy,

Captain Vere, and Claggart stand high in the hierarchy of natural man, above the limited comprehension of the mere worldly-wise. The last meeting of Vere and Budd is too sacred for the common view. "But there is no telling the sacrament, seldom if in any case revealed to the gadding world wherever under circumstances at all akin to those here attempted to be set forth two of great Nature's nobler order embrace." As to Claggart, his evil is an object of moral and aesthetic appreciation, a quality to be savored by connoisseurs.

To heighten and dignify the tragic action Melville, as in *Moby Dick* with Ahab, magnifies his characters by investing them in heroic myth, legend, and history. The background is "a crisis for Christendom not exceeded in its undetermined momentousness at the time by any other era of which there is record." The Handsome Sailor has mythical proportions. He is Aldebaran, a pagod, a grand Assyrian bull; at the yard-arm he is "young Alexander curbing the fiery Bucephalus. A superb figure, tossed up as by the horns of Taurus against the thunderous sky." He is Hercules refined by the influence of Venus, in him "something suggestive of a mother eminently favored by Love and the Graces." Melville thus states the problem of his modern tragedy:

> Passion, and passion in its profoundest, is not a thing demanding a palatial stage whereon to play its part. Down among the groundlings, among the beggars and rakers of the garbage, profound passion is enacted. And the circumstances that provoke it, however trivial or mean, are no measure of its power. In the present instance the stage is a scrubbed gun-deck, and one of the external provocations a man-of-war's man's spilled soup.

But his stage is so framed and so lighted as to display the tragic patterns to the best dramatic advantage. Antique myth, Christian allusion at its most spacious, and finally the aesthetic distance of a more poetic age of sail are all utilized to magnify and embellish. (One may remark here in passing that it is a waste of ingenuity to prove that Billy is not the Handsome Sailor. Insofar as the Sailor is mythic hero he cannot be, for this is not a man but an archetype. Billy is as close to being the Handsome Sailor as any human, closely scanned, is likely to get. How much use was Melville able to get out of Bulkington in *Moby Dick*?) One final comment upon magnification: there is a commemorative quality about *Billy Budd* which very interestingly fuses the tragedy of hero and common man, which blends the diverse tones of *Moby Dick* and *John Marr and Other Sailors*. It is a tale at once of Lord Nelson and of Greenwich pensioners, of mutiny, age-old oppression and pain, and of military splendor.

> To the mutineers those battles and especially Trafalgar were a plenary absolution; and a grand one; for all that goes to make up scenic naval

display and heroic magnificence in arms. Those battles especially Trafalgar stand unmatched in human annals.

Like classical tragedy, *Billy Budd* makes a clear distinction between the sphere of the actual and the sphere of the ideal. True judgment of Billy lies with natural law, here also divine, the realm of absolute justice—chronometrical, as Plotinus Plinlimmon would have it in *Pierre.* " 'At the last Assizes it shall acquit,' " says Vere. But Vere is equally clear on the distinction between a natural and a man-of-war world. The killing of Claggart is divine justice, but on the *Indomitable* it is the murder of a superior officer under wartime conditions. " 'Struck dead by an angel of God. Yet the angel must hang!' " " 'We proceed under the law of the Mutiny Act.' " In *Billy Budd* this tragic discrepancy is born of the dogma of the Fall of Man, which inevitably brings it into being. The law of the mutiny act is the law of a fallen world, in which an unfallen man like Billy cannot long exist. The immediate tragedy originates in a second Fall, the mutiny at the Nore, which has made any union of these worlds impossible. Age-old abuses of government, first rationally and properly protested at Spithead, have finally roused the "red meteor" of the Nore. "Reasonable discontent growing out of practical grievances in the fleet had been ignited into irrational combustion as by live cinders blown across the Channel from France in flames." The Revolution, one sees, is also a Fall. Many parallels with Melville's early writing have been suggested by critics of *Billy Budd.* At this point one might add to the list *The Encantadas,* and most particularly Sketch Seventh, "Charles's Isle and the Dog-King." The Encantadas are a fallen world in which no rational government can flourish, in which oppression on the one hand is countered on the other by unbridled license.

In still another respect *Billy Budd* follows the classic formula of tragedy. The mainspring of the plot is a reversal, the *peripateia* defined by Aristotle as a hallmark of the complex tragic action, in which carefully laid plans produce results directly opposite to expectation, with, if well-managed, an artistic effect of combined surprise and inevitability. Thus Vere's well-planned arrangements lead to the killing of Claggart and the execution of Billy. He is not, we recall, deceived by Claggart's accusation. He brings the two men privately to his cabin, in order to confront the liar with truth in a manner as little harmful as possible to the general welfare. He fully understands Billy's inability to speak, but by his very kindness he brings on the fatal blow. "Contrary to the effect intended, these words so fatherly in tone, doubtless touching Billy's heart to the quick, prompted yet more violent efforts at utterance—efforts soon ending for the time in confirming the paralysis, and bringing to the face an expression which was as a crucifixion to behold. The next instant, quick as the flame from a discharged cannon at night, his right arm shout out, and Claggart dropped to the deck." Inevitability accompanies surprise, as Aristotle has laid down, for Melville has carefully paved the way by his references to Billy's stutter—his one connection with a fallen world—and his sudden violence once before aboard the merchantman *Rights of Man.* " 'Quick as lightning Billy let fly his arm. I dare say he never meant to do quite as much as he did, but anyhow he gave the burly fool a terrible drubbing.' "

With so many of the traits and qualities of tragedy, *Billy Budd* can claim also the final attribute of tragic reconciliation. In his defeat and passion the tragic hero yet brings about a partial redemption, he keeps live some hope for the future, some confidence that goodness survives. So the story of Billy does not die, but is preserved and transmitted among seamen, and bits of the boom from which he was hanged are kept like pieces of the true Cross. This effect and survival of his memory might be contrasted with the effect of the announcement by Vere of Billy's impending execution, which "was listened to by the throng of standing sailors in a dumbness like that of a seated congregation of believers in hell listening to the clergyman's announcement of his Calvinistic text."

This reconciliation is not precisely Greek, nor yet the Hebraic catharsis of *Samson Agonistes*—"nothing is here to wail, nothing for tears." There is no firm base of belief on which to ground it. The system with which we are to be reconciled is too vast and ambiguous. In one dimension of meaning Captain Vere is certainly God the Father, as Billy is God the Son; but as Nathalia Wright has well remarked Vere is not omnipotent. He acts in accordance with a law that is not of his own framing. There is something beyond him. It would be interesting to compare other nineteenth-century experiments in meaning through myth, especially Byron's *Manfred,* in which level after level of the personified supernatural is tried and discarded, even Ahrimanes, the lord of all that is; or perhaps Shelley's *Prometheus Unbound,* in which Jupiter is eclipsed by the mighty shadow of Demogorgon, a formless, shapeless gloom.

As tragedy *Billy Budd* undoubtedly possesses tragic irony, the irony of fate. Its ironies would seem bitter to those who are inclined to view them bitterly. One might well think that Melville is presenting in *Billy Budd* a second crucifixion, which in this man-of-war world will inevitably be reenacted whenever Christ should reassume the estate of man. His irony, however, is the natural attitude of a capacious, energetic, and subtle mind in pursuit of as much meaning as it can grasp, and its honest admission of the presence in reality of a something finally ungraspable. It magnifies and intensifies, it deepens and enriches, rather than diminishing by a mere irony of wailing mockery. Viewed in the full context of the tragedy of *Billy Budd,* this irony is neither a scream nor a sneer.

# The Problem of *Billy Budd*

*by Edward H. Rosenberry*

When a monumental new edition of *Billy Budd* appeared in 1962, it was the hope of the editors that their exhaustive scholarship might contribute to a definitive interpretation of the novel. Such a wish might seem unnecessarily restrictive, but the extreme critical divergence on *Billy Budd* has created a genuine threat to its artistic integrity as a result of its apparent failure to support a demonstrable reading. This essay is an attempt to end the war, or to make the end more predictable. . . . The issues are intricately interconnected, since after all what we have to deal with is meaning in an organic work of art; but in as orderly a manner as possible I shall try to analyze the causes of critical error, as they appear to me, and then to show, by examining first the tone of the novel and then its ethical logic, that the plainest reading of this disputed book is the only valid reading possible.

## *I. Delusions*

A good starting point for this conservative case was provided several years ago by Richard Harter Fogle, who identified two "heresies" of *Billy Budd* criticism and dismissed them with entire justification, in my opinion, but without the formal refutation evidently needed to lay such stubborn ghosts.[2] He complained of the widespread attribution to Melville of an ironic tone resulting in a sardonic reversal of the story's ostensible meaning; and he complained particularly of Lawrance Thompson's invention (in *Melville's Quarrel with God*) of a quasi-authorial narrator in whose "bland" and "stupid" vision the apparent straightforwardness of the narration may be conveniently discounted. Thompson's idea is spectacular enough to deserve special mention, but it is basically the ironist heresy tricked out with a supporting device



[2] R. H. Fogle, "*Billy Budd:* The Order of the Fall," *Nineteenth Century Fiction,* XV (December 1960), 189–205.

which no other ironist has been clever enough to bring to his case. In effect, it only postpones the collapse of the case by one step, because there is no evidence that such a mediator between author and reader exists. Despite Wayne Booth's proper insistence on every author's "undramatized narrator" or "implicit second self,"[3] never altogether identical with the man behind the mask of art, a considerable burden of proof falls on the claim that these psychic twins are militantly opposed, and the obligation is not discharged by showing that the alter ego *must* be present if the meaning of the novel is to be reversed. Thompson's argument is simply circular and would perhaps have raised more general objection than it has if he had not invented also an "alert reader" who always adopts his views and with whom one is instinctively reluctant to dissociate himself. The real issue lies behind this little smoke screen: are we to take Melville at his word and read *Billy Budd* as a parable of the plight of innocence in a "man-of-war world," or are we to find beneath its tragic benediction a satiric attack on the complacency of earthly and heavenly authority?

Since the latter reading would render the novel, in Fogle's words, "cheap, puerile, and perverse" (witness *Pierre*), no one entertained that possibility until, in 1950, one adventurous essay[4] loosed a spate of ironist interpretations from the scholarly presses. The reasons for this, I am convinced, must be sought in the critics and their milieu rather than in the book. Wayne Booth makes the valuable point that a book tends to mean what we expect it to mean, "and the last several decades have produced—for whatever reasons—an audience that has been thrown off balance by a barrage of ironic works."[5] Irony-hunting has joined symbol-hunting as a fashionable indoor sport, which has so conditioned us to the expectation of obliquity and ambiguity that, as Booth says, "We can't accept a straight and simple statement when we read one." The popular mystique of close reading inclines us to see weasels in clouds and exposes contemporary criticism to what Plinlimmon would have called "strange, *unique* follies and sins." The most conspicuous of these in reading Melville is mistaking an occasional romantic petulance of temper for a considered philosophic posture.

In fact, our expectations of Melville constitute as real a source of error as did the very different expectations of his contemporaries. For them he was "the man who lived among the cannibals," and the leap from Typee to Saddle Meadows, or even to the try-works, was too much for them. For us he is the voice of Ahab and the Confidence-

[3] *The Rhetoric of Fiction*, pp. 151–152.

[4] Joseph Schiffman, "Melville's Final Stage, Irony: A Re-examination of *Billy Budd* Criticism," *American Literature*, XXII (May 1950), 128–136.

[5] *The Rhetoric of Fiction*, p. 366. The entire section labeled (after Saul Bellow) "Deep Readers of the World, Beware!" is worth reading on this topic.

Man, the sayer of "No! in thunder." We easily forget that the nay-saying he praised was Hawthorne's and not Beckett's or Sartre's, and that the remark was not made in *Billy Budd* or within thirty years of it. The ironist critics are at least partly disabled by the same prejudice that afflicts the anti-Stratfordians: the man in their minds could not possibly have written this work.

Reinforcing the *idée fixe* about the author is an equally powerful preconception of the characters in *Billy Budd*. The norms of the novel and the rhetoric that expresses them are clear enough in themselves, but they encounter resistance in the natural interests and sympathies of the reader. Booth has commented on the force in literature of "our irresistible sympathy for the innocent victim," [6] a sympathy so strongly generated by "Baby Budd" as to tempt the most wary of us (in Merlin Bowen's words) "to risk the luxury of at least following our own conscience." [7] Abetting this reaction is the equal and opposite inclination against Captain Vere. Melville, as I shall try to show, made Vere as attractive as he could in the face of his official austerity; but Billy, just as he stands, is an American Adam, loved from the start, and fit to be forgiven anything after he has struck his sacrificial blow at oppressive authority. We must resent his judge, irrespective of the merits of the case, on precisely the ground Melville once supposed to underlie the popular opinion of God: "The reason the mass of men fear God, and *at bottom dislike* Him, is because they rather distrust his heart, and fancy him all brain like a watch." [8] It is belief rather than disbelief which it is difficult to suspend in such a story as *Billy Budd*. Yet to be ruled by indignation, however righteous, is to subvert tragedy to melodrama. It happens to every freshman who lets himself be carried away by the "injured innocence" of Oedipus into the mistake of casting the oracle as villain. It is instructive to reflect on the critical abuse *Billy Budd* would deservedly draw if it really said what the ironists claim it says. *Weltschmerz* has never had much survival value as art.

Most pervasive of the fallacies I have noticed in the *Billy Budd* literature is the confusion of dramatic facts with the personal views of author or reader. . . .

[6] Ibid., p. 132. Booth is referring here specifically to Joyce's *Portrait of the Artist,* but the problem of sympathy is explored at large in Chs. v, ix, and x.

[7] Merlin Bowen, *The Long Encounter* (Chicago, 1960), p. 233. The full case against the argument from conscience will be made from another point of view further on.

[8] Letter to Hawthorne, June 1851.

## *II. Tone*

The assumption that a fictional character can be taken as a reliable spokesman for his author is boggy ground to build on. Yet somewhere within every successful fiction there must be adequate clues to that much-disputed but still indispensable value, the author's intention. What I mean by intention, let it be clear, is not belief but tone—that is, the belief-making mechanism of the story as we have it. Does the author's apparent attitude invite acceptance or rejection of the value system on which the story is based?

Some of the critical confusion which has beclouded *Billy Budd* has arisen out of an initial failure to define the "irony" which is supposed to throw its belief-making mechanism into reverse. So far as I know, R. H. Fogle is the only commentator to have illuminated this crucial point by observing that while *Billy Budd* is ironic enough in the Aristotelian sense (reversal of fortune, the "irony of fate"), it is not ironic in the rhetorical sense (reversal of meaning, the irony of satire).[9] Unhappily, the presence or absence of this latter irony is difficult to prove, and proof has so far been largely limited to assertion and counter-assertion. The critic peers into the text and sees, like Thurber at the microscope, his own eye. It helps, but it does not solve all problems, to say that irony is grounded in absurdity. In much contemporary literature absurdity is the norm, and even in fiction based on traditional norms the author's notion of what is out of joint, or his way of expressing it, may differ sharply from the reader's. One can only inspect what clues the text provides with an impartial eye and in the perspective of a scale of values as nearly exempt from the dangers of subjective manipulation as possible.

Much of the textual scrutiny has already been done piecemeal and only needs to be reviewed here.[10] There is first the fact of the novel's dedication to Jack Chase—simple, direct, reverent, memorializing the "great heart" of the most admirable man Melville had ever met. It may be, as Warner Berthoff has proposed, that this theme of magnanimity is the central strain of the narrative; at the very least it provides a keynote unmistakable in its sincerity and quite lacking in the ironic potential of the dedication of *Pierre* to Mount Greylock or of *Israel Potter* to the Bunker Hill monument.

[9] R. H. Fogle, "*Billy Budd*—Acceptance or Irony," *Tulane Studies in English*, VIII (1958), 109–110, 112.

[10] Among the many pertinent studies listed in the bibliography of Hayford and Sealts, I have found especially useful those of Berthoff (1960), Braswell (1957), Fogle (1958, 1960), and Miller (1958). A very important contribution of W. G. Kilbourne, Jr., will be discussed in another connection.

This keynote is consistently echoed in Melville's portrayal of his principals. Capping his introductory sketch of Captain Vere in Chapter vii, Melville emphasizes that natures like Vere's are rare in that "honesty prescribes to them directness." Characterizing the common seaman in Chapter xvi, he writes with simple nostalgia of the "old-fashioned sailor" whose "frankness" stands in contrast to the landsman's "finesse," "long head," "indirection," and "distrustfulness." In describing the life ashore Melville anticipates our popular concept of gamesmanship: "an oblique, tedious, barren game hardly worth that poor candle burnt out in playing it." In the following chapter he appeals for acceptance of his simple protagonist by disarming the anticipated skepticism of the sophisticated reader and demanding in its place "something else than mere shrewdness." His only devious and ironical character is the villain Claggart, and to him he has Captain Vere say, "Be direct, man." Here, in short, is an internal scale of values as poorly contrived to nourish an ironic tone as can well be imagined.[11]

As the story develops, it becomes steadily plainer that the irony is all in the case and not in the author's attitude toward it. Into his climactic episode in Chapter xxi Melville built a classic Aristotelian irony by which "innocence and guilt . . . changed places" and it became a fact as unalterable as the parricide of Oedipus that Billy had killed an officer in performance (however badly) of his duty. Then, in the next breath, Melville extended his *donnée* to include the inevitable judgment of the captain, who "was not authorized to determine the matter on [the] primitive basis [of] essential right and wrong." At the end of the chapter, as a further inducement to our acceptance of that decision, he appended a warning to the "snug card players in the cabin" not to pass judgment on the actions "under fire" of "the sleepless man on the bridge." In the face of such rhetoric one might rather expect to find an author reproached for excessive explicitness than debated as an enigma.

On the other hand, if it seems impossible for the ironists to be right, it is not wholly their fault that they are wrong. The seal of reconciliation which the condemned Billy is made to place upon his captain's intransigent sentence is mystical and as hard to accept as the forgiveness of Christ on the cross. On such a scene as their final interview in Chapter xxii, the author felt obliged to draw the curtain and to content himself with hinting at the passionate consonance supposed to have welled up in the spirits of these two "phenomenal" natures. His allusion to them as Abraham and Isaac is a clue to both his sincerity and his difficulty. The originals are accepted (when they are accepted)

[11] Some of this very evidence is used by Wayne Booth, p. 178, in citing *Billy Budd* as an example of "reliable" narration.

by a suspension of disbelief in which poetic faith is immeasurably assisted by religious faith. Melville can only invoke his biblical counterparts by allusion and hope for the best. That he fears the worst, however, is apparent from the nervous manner in which he reminds us of the "rarer qualities" in the natures of his "Abraham" and "Isaac"—"so rare indeed as to be all but incredible to average minds however much cultivated." This is diffidence, and well founded, but not irony. Melville is not mocking belief but pleading for it. The ironists are simply those readers with whom his appeal has failed. . . .

The reader who dismisses Vere as a shallow formalist is taking part of Melville's *donnée* for the whole. When Vere proclaims his unalterable allegiance to the King's "buttons," it is possible to think of him simply as a man in a sailor suit, "accustomed," as Melville describes the species in Chapter xvi, "to obey orders without debating them." What must be kept in mind is the hard prior debate inside "Starry" Vere which could alone persuade a thoughtful man to don the King's buttons in the first place. What was threatened in the Nore Mutiny, Melville reminds us in Chapter iii, was not just naval authority but "the flag of founded law and freedom defined." It is this symbol to which Vere has sworn his difficult allegiance, an allegiance reaffirmed in his disputed reflections at the close of Chapter xxvii on the human need for "measured forms." Like Hobbes, Vere sees unbridled man as a beast, and law (in Melville's provocative image) as "Orpheus with his lyre spellbinding the wild denizens of the wood."

Legality as music is a figure seemingly out of keeping with the harsh spirit of that "child of War," the Mutiny Act. Yet in a world in which mutiny is a serviceable metaphor for the moral and theological condition of man, an imposed order is the only kind that is possible, and the articles under which Captain Vere takes his authority are not radically different from those under which Moses took his. With respect to the taking of life, neither the military nor the biblical statute goes beyond a general prohibition. The extenuations of circumstance, as Melville well knew, are as infinitely adjustable as the "Protean easy-chair" of the Confidence-Man, built to "ease human suffering [by] endlessly changeable accommodations" in which "the most tormented conscience must, somehow and somewhere, find rest." *Billy Budd,* I contend, was conceived as the kind of story in which such accommodations are not available. It invites comparison in its ethical structure, not to "The Birthmark," the one tale of Hawthorne to which Melville acknowledged a specific debt, but to *The Scarlet Letter.* Both stories deal with the collision of private morality and the law in a tight little community which admits no extenuations. They have a number of features in common—a devil figure, self-destroyed; a child of nature, innocent but flawed—but most importantly a central sensibility impaled on a dilemma precisely defined by the opposition of statutory and romantic law. Billy's exoneration, like Dimmesdale's marriage, is made in heaven but can only be recognized there. One irreducible fact gets all but lost in the personal sympathy generated by both characters: no law can sanction the execution of bad officers by their men or the extra-marital intercourse of clergymen with their parishioners.

Vere has been abused for his instant observation that "the angel must hang," as though he were prejudging Billy and making a mockery of his trial. But it is hard to see how such a sentiment can prevail in any reasoned estimate of the story. If one sees a man commit murder, one knows that he ought to suffer the penalty; and one also knows that in a civilized society the guilt, however obvious, must be determined and the penalty exacted by due process. Vere's remark may sound unsportsmanlike, but it cannot be regarded as unjust. If he blunders at all at this point, it is not in anticipating judgment but in assessing character. Here and here only he displays prejudice: he likes Billy and dislikes Claggart. The reader allows him these feelings because he shares them and has privileged information which justifies them. But Vere does not have this information and decides on intuition alone that he has seen an "Ananias . . . struck dead by an angel of God." If Claggart were a sympathetic character, our indignation would be justly turned against the superior who treated him with peremptory contempt, was prepared to take a subordinate's word against his, and laid him open to a judgment which not only preceded but precluded trial. The death of Claggart is exactly like that of a soldier Montaigne tells of in "Of Conscience" (II.v), whose stomach was cut open to determine whether he had stolen food as charged. It appeared that he had, but, as Montaigne ironically remarked, what "an instructive condemnation!"

Unwittingly Vere misleads us in the direction of allegory. His word "angel" too effectively polarizes the principals of the drama in his cabin. It is a touch of romance which we can surely forgive in a character sometimes thought to lack heart; but it increases difficulty for both himself and the reader. Forgetting the patent symbolism of Billy's stammer and the reality of the crime it makes him commit, and ignoring Melville's explicit disclaimer of romantic intentions (end of Chapter ii), we are apt to mistake a human tragedy for the Death of Innocence in a morality play. And the tendency is aggravated by an equal and opposite gravitation, dramatized by the officers of the court, toward compromise rather than categorical decision in the matter of punishment. What shouldn't happen to a dog is happening to an "angel," and we quarrel with that uncongenial part of the author's *donnée* expressed in Vere's indubitable mandate to "condemn or let go."

. . . Seen in this light, Vere's problem is one of moral navigation, and its solution is dictated by a respect for his charts which is both characteristic and heroic.

. . . It is not sneering at the great body of *Billy Budd* criticism to suggest, in conclusion, that it has expressed bewilderment. It is only saying that some very good thinking has chosen some very bad grounds. Unlike "The Lady or the Tiger?" *Billy Budd* was never conceived as a puzzle for our solution or a choice for our decision, but rather as a course of events for our contemplation. Unfortunately, the polemical virus runs strong in the scholar–critic, and the natural effect of being drawn into the story is to take sides on its warring values. A firm will is needed to remember, with Tindall, that *Billy Budd* is "not a conclusion, like a sermon, [but] a vision of confronting what confronts us, of man thinking things out with all the attendant confusions and uncertainties." [12] This is a Sophoclean Melville in *Billy Budd,* speaking with a detachment and a respect for fact that criticism must emulate if it is to get at his meaning.

[12] William York Tindall, "The Ceremony of Innocence," *Great Moral Dilemmas in Literature,* ed. R. M. MacIver (New York, 1956), p. 80. [Tindall's essay is reprinted in this volume, pp. 34–40—Ed.]

# The Tragedy of Justice in *Billy Budd*

*by Charles A. Reich*

The divine law of the Last Assizes, a law that judges the totality of man, is beyond human ability to administer; more, it is beyond human ability to *imagine*. Such justice must ever remain unknowable to humans. When Claggart, the lying Ananias, is killed, Vere exclaims "Struck dead by an angel of God! Yet the angel must hang!" But this is no paradox. Men cannot enforce divine judgments.

Human law must accept the fact that the mind is largely unknowable; that motives can seldom be ascertained. How are we to judge a man who kills because he *thought* the other was threatening his life, or because he *thought* the other had killed his child, or because he *thought* God had commanded him to do the act? In such cases, the law ordinarily resorts to some objective test of the supposed state of mind. In a case of self-defense, we do not simply ask the killer what he thought at the time. We seek to determine on an objective basis whether the victim was actually approaching with a weapon in circumstances where the killer had no reasonable opportunity to escape. Provocation must likewise be determined not only by reference to the state of mind of the person provoked (he may be hypersensitive, or even paranoid) but by an objective look at the nature of the provocation. To some extent all law, and even more so the military law, "looks but to the frontage, the appearance." In sum, human law looks primarily to men's actions, the one objective reality that is presented. Human law says that men are *defined* by their acts; they are the sum total of their actions, and no more.

In this light, the initial conflict in *Billy Budd* can be reassessed. Billy is not innocent in the sense in which that term is used in resolving issues of justice. Billy is innocent in what he is, not what he does. The opposite of his Miltonic type of innocence is not guilt, but experience. The conflict is not a "catastrophe of innocence"; it is a conflict between society and Nature that contains—even in Billy's case—both good and evil. It is a "catastrophe of Nature." His inability to adapt to society is the inability of nature to be civilized. Billy is incapable of acquiring experience. And the failing that leads to his execution is his incapacity to use the civilized man's weapon of speech. In society, natural forces cannot fight out their battles; Billy cannot use his physical strength to strike back at Claggart. The novel, then, is not an analysis of Billy or of Claggart. Instead, it asks the question *how did it fare* with Billy in the year of the Great Mutiny? With this question framed, our interest turns to the responses that are made to this encounter.

The chief agent of the law is Captain Vere. It is his decision that dooms Billy, and many critics have blamed him: they have suggested that Vere is everything from a conscientious but rigid military disciplinarian to an unprincipled autocrat—that the summoning of a drumhead court was unnecessary or illegal; that Vere acted impulsively; that Vere's approach to the law, and to the possibility of mitigation, was either expedient or rigid and unimaginative; that Vere may even have been temporarily affected in his mind (as the surgeon suggests). But not only is this blame misplaced, it obscures the drama that takes place in Vere's consciousness—a drama that is crucial to the novel's development.

At the outset, it is vital to note that Melville allows Vere no choice within the terms of the law itself; if the law is obeyed, Billy must hang. It is quite true that criminal law can be far more flexible than the Mutiny Act. Under modern law Billy would not receive a death penalty; he would probably get a relatively short prison sentence. But that is not the kind of law that Melville gives us. We are told that under the Mutiny Act a mere blow to a superior, regardless of its effect, is a capital offense, and the law provides no exceptions for palliating circumstances. "Budd's intent or non-intent is nothing to the purpose." Could Vere have mitigated the penalty? While the question is not wholly free from doubt, the answer seems to be no. Vere begins his answer to this question, addressed to him by the lieutenant, by saying "were that clearly lawful for us under the circumstances," the implication clearly being that it is not. The efforts at compromise must therefore be rejected. The court must "condemn or let go."

Vere did have the option of holding the case for the admiral, instead of summoning his own drumhead court. Vere, we are told, "fain would" have submitted the case to the admiral. But as a true military officer he kept to his vows of allegiance to martial duty; and here the urgency of preventing any slumbering embers of the Nore Mutiny from igniting among the crew overruled for him every other consideration. By hindsight, we can surmise that the danger did not exist. But are we entitled to judge the actions of a military commander in wartime by hindsight?

The narrator's answer is unequivocal. He argues that forty years after the event we cannot reason how a battle should have been fought, nor second-guess other emergencies when it was imperative promptly to act. "Little ween the snug cardplayers in the cabin of the responsibilities of the sleepless man on the bridge." We may perhaps criticize the law, but not the officer whose "vowed responsibility" is to "adhere to it and administer it."

Moreover, the Mutiny Act, however unreasonable it may seem today, was accepted as the norm by those aboard the *Bellipotent.* Vere says:

> The people [meaning the ship's company] have native sense; most of them are familiar with our naval usage and tradition, and how would they take it? Even could you explain to them—which our official position forbids—they, long molded by arbitrary discipline, have not that kind of intelligent responsiveness that might qualify them to comprehend and discriminate. No, to the people the foretopman's deed, however it be worded in the announcement, will be plain homicide committed in a flagrant act of mutiny.

Clearly, then, *Billy Budd* is designed to give us a case where compromise is impossible, and where Vere, and we, are forced to confront the imperatives of law. As Melville presents the case, there is no escape for Vere. It is in this light that we must appreciate Vere's reactions.

Vere, as he is described to us, is no deranged zealot or unfeeling automaton, but a very superior and very human man. Although a man of settled convictions, his objection to novel ideas was not due to moral blindness—rather "because they seemed to him insusceptible of embodiment in lasting institutions, but at war with the peace of the world and the true welfare of mankind." More than this, Vere was a man of unusual sensitivity, one who, unlike many judges, could imaginatively perceive the truth about Billy's nature and state of mind. When Billy and Claggart confront each other, and Billy cannot answer or defend himself, Vere immediately divines Billy's liability to vocal impediment. Later, when Billy is asked by the court to explain why Claggart so maliciously lied, Vere understands that Billy lacks the sophistication to explain. And when Billy declares, "I have eaten the King's bread and I am true to the King," Vere exclaims "I believe you, my man." Far from being a military ramrod, "something exceptional in the moral quality of Captain Vere made him, in earnest encounter with a fellow man, a veritable touchstone of that man's essential nature." The reader may, in fact, surmise that Vere realizes as well as we do how hard is the role he is fated to play.

Moreover, Vere is from the first deeply affected by Billy. The narrator of Vere:

> Though in general not very demonstrative to his officers, he had congratulated Lieutenant Ratcliffe upon his good fortune in lighting upon

> such a fine specimen of the genus homo, who in the nude might have posed for a statue of young Adam before the Fall.

Is the description of Billy in this sentence an intrusion of the author, or is it what it seems to be—a statement of Vere's own feelings? We are reminded of the feelings of Billy's other captain, the master of the *Rights-of-Man,* when Billy was taken away from him: " 'Ay, Lieutenant, you are going to take away the jewel of 'em; you are going to take away my peacemaker!' And with that the good soul had really some ado in checking a rising sob." But in Vere there is something deeper. Billy is some ways a son to the childless Captain. Several times, in his dealings with Billy, Vere is described as fatherly, and this aspect of Vere is recognized by the orphan Billy, "doubtless touching Billy's heart to the quick."

How does Vere react to the encounter between Billy and the law? As we first meet Vere, he is a man of "settled convictions," who doubtless accepts law quite unthinkingly; he is also a man whose humanity is closely confined: "the most undemonstrative of men." But from the moment that Billy strikes his fateful blow, we see Vere changing. When Vere first realizes what the consequences of Billy's act must be, Vere becomes so excited and convulsed that the self-poised surgeon, who has never before seen the Captain like this, is himself "profoundly discomposed." The surgeon almost supposes Vere to have lost his reason. Later, when Billy testifies that he has been true to the King, Vere exclaims that he believes Billy, Vere's "voice indicating a suppressed emotion not otherwise betrayed." Soon after, Vere interrupts the testimony in such a way as "to augment a mental disturbance previously evident enough." And at one point in his argument to the court, Vere implies his own inner state when he says, "To steady us a bit, let us recur to the facts." After the decision, Vere himself communicates the judgment to Billy. The narrator surmises that Vere, in his last interview with Billy, may have developed a passion latent under his stoical exterior, and finally caught Billy to his heart, "letting himself melt back into what remains primeval in our formalized humanity." When Vere emerges, his face is "expressive of the agony of the strong," and the narrator suggests that "the condemned one suffered less than he who mainly had effected the condemnation." When, at the penultimate moment, Billy cries out, "God bless Captain Vere," "Vere, either through stoic self-control or a sort of momentary paralysis induced by emotional shock, stood erectly rigid as a musket in the ship-armorer's rack." Vere has been condemned for being a ramrod, but quite plainly he stands like a musket in order to control the feelings within him. Vere's death comes not long after Billy's. And just as Billy dies with Vere's name on his lips, so Vere's last recorded words are "Billy Budd, Billy Budd."

We see two things at work here. First is the growth of Vere's consciousness and humanity, all the more notable for the fact that Vere is the only character in the book who visibly changes. It is not the pedantic Vere of the opening who finally embraces Billy. Second, Vere comes to recognize that there are values beyond those which the law embodies. It is not that Vere ever gets so far as to question the law itself; clearly he does not. But he does learn—and this is the vital point—that if the law is to be followed, other values must be sacrificed; in this case, the life of "a fellow creature innocent before God." It is for this reason that he calls the law pitiless, and that he finally realizes that to obey the law he must reject not only the urgings of his heart, "but also the conscience, the private conscience." Private conscience, he says, "must yield to the imperial one."

Thus Captain Vere is shown not as the protagonist of the law, but as a man faced with an awful choice. Because he is a man in and of society, because he occupies a position of duty and responsibility, he chooses the law, however inadequate it may be. Echoing the words of Lord Coleridge, he says: "But the exceptional in the matter moves the hearts within you. Even so too mine is moved. But let not warm hearts betray heads that should be cool. Ashore in a criminal case, will an upright judge allow himself off the bench to be waylaid by some tender kinswoman of the accused seeking to touch him with her tearful plea? Well, the heart here, sometimes the feminine in man, is as that piteous woman, and hard though it be, she must here be ruled out."

Although this complex and subtle portrait of Vere is essential to *Billy Budd,* it is not in itself the central concern of the novel. It is, rather, a means to bring us to the central problem. Melville has shown us a law whose logic is impeccable, and yet made us feel that the law has terrible shortcomings. What is wrong with the law? What is wrong with society, the law's progenitor? It is these questions that the novel ultimately asks.

However deep Vere's feelings may be, his vision is sharply circumscribed, for he is not privileged to observe events at a distance but must act. And after we have glimpsed his humanity, we are reminded that his understanding is limited; his last comments are that "forms, measured forms, are everything," and this is the only lesson he draws from "the story of Orpheus with his lyre spellbinding the wild denizens of the wood." We, however, are allowed to witness events through the eyes of observers, and as observers ourselves, and thus we are invited to look beyond Vere's range of vision.

After the judging of Billy and the dilemma of the judge comes the climax—the execution. It is a truly extaordinary scene, a formal, solemn act of society which every onlooker regrets. It is as if society has become a will separate from the will of all of its members. Vere himself stands in a state of shock. The members of the court other than Vere are deeply troubled. The surgeon is full of misgiving. The chaplain is certain that Billy belongs in heaven. As for the crew, they receive the announcement of Billy's crime and forthcoming punishment "in a dumbness like that of a seated congregation of believers in hell listening to the clergyman's announcement of his Calvinistic text." At the execution, after a moment of silence, an inarticulate murmur passes through the men like a fresh torrent advancing through precipitous woods, a wordless sound of pouring mountain showers.

Nor does the narrator accept the execution without implicit protest. Although he describes himself as an old man and affects a mood of meditative distance from the events he relates, he frequently makes comments that suggest his feelings are not so serene as his manner. To cite one of many examples, he says that the chaplain is lending "the sanction of the religion of the meek to that which practically is the abrogation of everything but brute force." Even stronger feelings are implied by the narrator's many descriptions of Billy. Far from being a purely symbolic character, Billy is made very alive and very human. The narrator needs only a few swift brush strokes to bring Billy to life: Billy's cheerful salute to his old ship ("And goodbye to you too, old *Rights-of-Man*"), his affectionate and humorous respect for the salty old Dansker, his impulsive thanks to Captain Vere. Despite a pose as philosophical observer, the narrator betrays a passionate intensity of feeling when he speaks of the Handsome Sailor. In contrast to the Dansker, who regards Billy with "a certain grim internal merriment," the narrator is obviously deeply moved by the rare goodness of the young sailor.

Moreover, the execution scene presents its own elements that question the law, for in the end the scene is one of transcendence. The sky is "shot through with a soft glory as of the fleece of the lamb of God seen in mystical vision"; Billy ascends; his body does not struggle but by some prodigy reposes while suspended in the air; his form takes the full rose of the dawn. The sailors make a legend of Billy, and it is their ballad about him, "Billy in the Darbies," which ends the book.

How are we to understand this scene? It does not challenge the law that forbids one man to kill another; as to this commandment a mood of acceptance seems to prevail. What the scene does challenge is how society enforces this rule. Because Billy has unintentionally killed, must he be utterly destroyed? The focus of our anguish in *Billy Budd* is not Billy's innocence but the rejection of human values symbolized by his punishment.

Seeing Billy hanged, we are compelled to question whether Billy's punishment accomplishes any purpose at all. Certainly nothing is accomplished with respect to Billy; fear of punishment did not deter him, and even if the sentence were not capital, it is difficult to see what he could be expected to learn. Nor is the punishment useful in curbing mutinous tendencies among the crew; as we are shown, Billy's execution is far more likely to cause mutiny than to quell it.

The problem of punishment brings us back to the case of Dudley and Stephens. It is a commonplace assumption that punishment is necessary to make people obey. But Dudley and Stephens knew very well that murder was punishable by death under the law of England, and perhaps they believed in divine punishment as well, for they asked God's forgiveness. Nevertheless, they killed. No punishment, no matter how severe, can possibly deter men from eating one another if this offers their only chance of survival. Nor is punishment likely to reform or rehabilitate in such circumstances; until starvation forced them to crime there is nothing we know of in Dudley and Stephens that required reform or rehabilitation, and their experience is not one which they would have been likely to want to repeat. At first glance the case of Dudley and Stephens seems to present a unique situation. But the more that we know about the causes of criminal behavior, the more the predicament of Dudley and Stephens seems to be the predicament of most criminals. Crime stems from family background and upbringing, environment (especially slum environment), character disorder, mental illness, overwhelming circumstances, and the like. The individual who commits a cirme is responding to the forces of a separate universe. For one person that universe may be an unbearable family situation leading to violence, for another, a subculture in which criminal behavior is the norm rather than the exception, as shown in Claude Brown's *Manchild in the Promised Land* and in Oscar Lewis's *The Children of Sanchez.* More often than not, the universe from which the crime derives is isolated from the influence of society as a whole, precisely as in the Dudley and Stephens case. That case, rather than being unique, is virtually a paradigm of the criminal situation. It is exceptional, however, because in its unique circumstances we can clearly see the forces that made criminals out of ordinary men, while in the usual case we cannot or will not see them. And it was doubtless because of this special clarity that even the government of Queen Victoria was able for once to see the uselessness of execution and to commute the sentences.

The law forbids acts, while punishment destroys the whole man. But, as Melville shows, in human beings, as in nature, we cannot expect perfection. Early in his story, the narrator tells us that

> Billy was a striking instance that the arch interferer, the envious marplot of Eden, still has more or less to do with every human consignment to

> this planet of Earth. In every case, one way or another he is sure to slip in his little card, as much as to remind us—I too have a hand here.

But society has not learned how to deal with man as a flawed creature. Like the Benthamites, it is narrowly "scientific" or rational, and thus makes a profound error. Society, in its morality and in its laws, insists upon a black and white dichotomy. Men are either good or evil; the law must "condemn or let go."

It is this limited and inadequate view of human nature which is exposed by the most brilliant turn of the story: the ironic reversal of roles between Billy and Claggart. By presenting a man whose character is almost perfectly good, and another who is almost pure evil, the story forces upon our sensibilities the inadequacy of society's formal understanding of man.

> In the jugglery of circumstances preceding and attending the event on board the *Bellipotent* and in the light of that martial code whereby it was formally to be judged, innocence and guilt personified in Claggart and Budd in effect changed places. . . . Yet more. The essential right and wrong involved in the matter, the clearer that might be, so much the worse for the responsibility of a loyal sea commander, inasmuch as he was not authorized to determine the matter on that primitive basis.

In Billy's case, the law is unable to distinguish the human being from his act. The act is a guilty one, but does that mean that an individual whose life has been the purest goodness must be cast out forever? Billy is treated by the law as if he were no longer human, as if it is necessary for all others to distance themselves from him. But the onlookers retain their knowledge of Billy's humanity, and for them—and for us—the spectacle of his destruction is all but impossible to bear. Billy's execution is thus an image of society's failure to make its actions fit its understanding. Society's spiritual knowledge of man is far in advance of its laws. Time after time in the novel compassion and understanding struggle to break through the forms. The onlookers know what Billy is—even the sailors feel that he is morally incapable of malice. But the onlookers do not know how else to deal with his transgression. Hence they permit and participate in an action that destroys a fellow man and dehumanizes them all. This disparity of knowledge and action is perfectly embodied in the chaplain: he accepts all of society's forms, but when taking leave of the condemned fellow, "he kissed on the fair cheek his fellow man."

Indeed, from the moment of Billy's impulsive blow we feel caught in a process of insane logic that, once under way, proceeds to its final conclusion despite the better judgment of all concerned. The logic is faultless within its own terms, but the terms fall short. The law's insanity is like that earlier attributed to Claggart: although apparently subject to reason, it is deeply irrational. "Toward the accomplishment of an aim which in wantonness of malignity would seem to partake of the insane, he will direct a cool judgment sagacious and sound." Such madness "is to the average mind not distinguishable from sanity, and for the reason above suggested: that, whatever its aims may be—and the aim is never declared—the method and outward proceeding are always perfectly rational." The law, designed to be the protector of man's highest aspirations against the savagery of nature, has become instead the irrational destroyer of man.

*Billy Budd* is directly concerned with the law, but its broader concern is with society as a whole. Melville's novel shows how little the formal actions of society are adapted to the compound of good and evil which we know to be the essence of man's humanity. Civilization, in fact, is equated with blindness. "Nay, in an average man of the world, his constant rubbing with it blunts that finer spiritual insight indispensable to the understanding of the essential in certain exceptional characters, whether evil ones or good." Law, we are told, hardly sheds "so much light into obscure spiritual places as the Hebrew prophets." This blindness is illustrated by society's picture of Billy as shown by the newspaper account: a depraved criminal. The newspaper article grotesquely mimics the way in which the law views Billy and deals with him, and in the book it perfectly represents society's inability to comprehend or to accept natural man.

Throughout the novel Melville sets off the Natural against the formal artificiality of intellect and civilization. There is, for example, the symbolic but vital matter of speech versus gesture. All of the characters are at their most human when they gesture rather than speak: Vere when he embraces Billy, the sailors when they murmur wordlessly at the execution, the chaplain accompanying Billy, "the genuine gospel . . . less on his tongue than in his aspect and manner toward him." Billy, illiterate and subject to an infirmity of speech, is wholly natural.

The theme of the richness of humanity versus narrow utilitarianism is also the point of the much debated passage on Lord Nelson early in the book. The passage contrasts steel with firearms, knightly valor with ungallant modern warfare, and the oldtime ships, grand, picturesque, and poetic, with the unsightly ironclads. As for Nelson himself, that gloriously un-utilitarian sailor, he is a heroic counterpart of Billy. Like Billy, Nelson dies because of the natural qualities in him, his reckless valor and display, qualities disparaged by the narrow-minded "martial utilitarians," those "Benthamites of war." As Melville said in his poem, "A Utilitarian View of the Monitor's Fight":

> No passion; all went on by crank,
>     Pivot and screw,

> And calculations of caloric. . . .
> War yet shall be, but warriors
> Are now but operatives. . . .

This theme is sounded with a soaring affirmation of the grandeur of natural man in contrast to the utilitarian rationality of society. Billy, the natural man, is not only good, he is regal. The Handsome Sailor receives the homage and love of his shipmates; he is young Alexander, "A superb figure, tossed up . . . against the thunderous sky." Here Melville seems to return at the end of his life to the romance of his youth, to *Typee* and *Omoo* and the full life of nature. In contrast, society is a poor and artificial thing.

> The character marked by such qualities has to an unvitiated taste an untampered-with flavor like that of berries, while the man thoroughly civilized even in a fair specimen of the breed has to the same moral palate a questionable smack as of a compounded wine.

> The sailor is frankness, the landsman is finesse. Life is not a game with the sailor, demanding the long head—no intricate game of chess where few moves are made in straightforwardness and ends are attained by indirection, an oblique, tedious, barren game hardly worth that poor candle burnt out in playing it.

Billy indeed is, ironically, the true civilizer. For while the war in which the *Bellipotent* fights is the product of what passes for civilization, Billy is the maker of peace. "Billy came and it was like a Catholic priest striking peace in an Irish shindy . . . a virtue went out of him, sugaring the sour ones . . . they all love him . . . and it's the happy family here."

"Billy in the Darbies," a picture of Billy dreaming and awaiting death in the iron fetters of the law, is not only the ending of the novel, it was also its beginning, for Melville first wrote the poem, and then the novel. In essence, the poem is a question: Why is Billy to be hanged from the yardarm-end; why is he to be dropped "Fathoms down, fathoms down"? And just as the poem is a question, so the entire book is a question. In telling Billy's story Melville is asking about the fate of the natural in man. There are some who have found in Melville's book a mood of peace, and they are right, for Melville seemingly had made peace with the old warring elements of good and evil in nature that obsessed him in *Moby Dick*. It is as if Melville has finally accepted the antinomies of good and evil as being essential parts of fully realized life. But the overall mood of *Billy Budd* is not peaceful, for Melville at the end of his life is wondering whether youth, feeling, and love can survive into the drabness of a civilization dominated by material and organizational values. It is like the question he asked obliquely in *Bartleby the Scrivener,* where civilization isolates the man of perverse but genuine independence. It is the same question he asked in the Civil War poem, "On the Slain Collegians," where civilization's single-minded cold logic sends its ardent boys to death:

> Like plants that flower ere comes the leaf—
> Which storms lay low in kindly doom,
> And kill them in their flush of bloom.

*Billy Budd* is an intensely modern novel. It is concerned with the coming of a materialist, commercial civilization, rational and scientific, in which society grows ever more distant from the rich overflowing of human experience. Billy harks back to a more adventurous and youthful America which, with the frontier and the whaleship, was already passing in Melville's lifetime. Billy's type comes from "the time before steamships," the significant words with which the novel opens.

Melville's last book is a pessimistic view of America's destiny. But the novel does not have a conclusion. As Melville himself says, it lacks an "architectural finial." It looks ahead. Just as Billy, in death, transcends the limitations of the ship's world, so the novel, through the medium of art, transcends the world of Melville's day. For us in this day, the novel is a reminder of the indispensable importance of the artistic vision in the structuring of society—an expression of the need for society to accept the natural in man. Law, as a *creation* of man, needs the imagination and the insight of art so that it is not drawn in such a way as to imprison the human spirit. Law and society need the help of the artist, to the end that we do not forget man's natural humanity, which is embodied, timelessly and unforgettably, in "the fresh young image of the Handsome Sailor."

# The Example of *Billy Budd*

*by Werner Berthoff*

The ground common to most discussion of *Billy Budd* is the assumption that the story is allegorical—a narrative representation of some universal truth or law or balance of contraries, a parable of Good and Evil, a re-enactment of the Fall, a projected myth of a ritual killing which is also a resurrection, and so on. Such interpretations do not have to be scrambled for. The evidence they adduce is undeniably there. The trouble is rather that the statement of them will seem to miss what one feels, as one reads and re-reads, to be the governing concentration and emphasis of the actual telling. *Billy Budd* is indeed full of quickening intimations as to the larger, the perhaps universal circumstance of human life—intimations which are typical of Melville's imagination, as his explicitness in articulating them is typical of his best performance as a writer. But the decisive narrative logic and cogency of the story are, I think, to be found elsewhere. They are to be found in an effort which Melville characteristically troubled to furnish precise words for, the effort to "define and denominate certain phenomenal men" (Chapter 11). To render in force and detail through all the incident and commentary of his narrative the essential feature and bearing of these men, to name and make authoritative the example of character manifested in them—this is what seems to me to lie at the heart of Melville's enterprise. In *Billy Budd* he undertakes to define not universal truth but certain specific and contingent examples of being and behavior.

This undertaking is not to be felt in equal force at every point in the story. In the opening chapters a reader looking into *Billy Budd* for the first time, without benefit of editorial introductions but with some knowledge of Melville's earlier books, would be very likely to suppose that he had come upon another *Israel Potter*. Melville (as a study of his manuscript changes makes evident) had his difficulties in determining the best use of his materials and in discovering the proper drift

---

*"The Example of* Billy Budd.*" From* The Example of Melville *by Werner Berthoff (Princeton, N. J.: Princeton University Press, 1962), pp. 194–203.* 

and consequence of his story. In some respects his problem, though on a different scale, resembles that of Hardy a few years later in *The Dynasts*: both works, looking back a century to the strange apocalyptic wars of a long-vanished time, are not unconcerned with the particular ideological issues of that time; yet both mean to place the ultimate causes and meaning of the events recorded in the working of less contingent forces. So *Billy Budd* opens with several chapters on the historical background—the war with revolutionary France, the naval mutinies—and repeatedly turns aside to show how this bears upon the action. In fact, Melville goes further and introduces or intimates what might seem to be even more restrictive considerations, aligning Captain Vere (and himself as narrator) with a philosophic anti-Jacobinism, calling one ship the *Rights-of-Man* and another the *Athéiste*, and so forth. All this is clearly meant to inform the story. But it is not meant to explain the story. The historical circumstances touch on the story at every crisis but do not essentially determine it. We are to feel both elements, the framing conditions and the special action, as real and consequential; the era intensifies our sense of the event as the event substantiates our impression of the era; but each is to be apprehended as following its own logic. The trouble is that if we respond at all to the impressive terms and symbols Melville used to embody his story, we may press upon them too rigid or predetermined an arrangement; we may be misled (as E. M. Forster cautioned with regard to *Moby-Dick*) "into harmonizing the incidents" and so screen out the distinguishing "roughness and richness" of the narrative as a whole.[1]

## II

I do not mean to dismiss out of hand the various allegorical interpretations of *Billy Budd*. If only in their striking variety and equal conviction, they have much to tell us—about the nature of Melville's writing as well as about the excitements and hazards of criticism. No one has worked along this line of approach more discerningly than Professor Norman Holmes Pearson, whose findings have the merit of standing near the center of sensible opinion on the story and may serve briefly—I hope not unfairly—as a stalking horse.[2] To Professor Pear-

[1] *Aspects of the Novel* (New York, 1927), p. 200.

[2] "*Billy Budd:* 'The King's Yarn,'" *American Quarterly*, III (Summer 1951), 99–114. Justification for the diversity of critical comment *Billy Budd* has given rise to is suggested by the penetrating judgment of the poet Montale, that the story is at one and the same time an epic, a tale of adventure, a Platonic dialogue, a critical essay, and a mystery play: "An Introduction to *Billy Budd*" (1942), *Sewanee Review*, LXVII (Summer 1960), 410–411.

son, *Billy Budd* is best understood by analogy to Milton's heroic poems: "What Melville was doing was to try to give in as universalized a way as possible . . . another redaction of the myth which had concerned Milton . . . in the trilogy of his three major works"—the Christian myth, that is, of the fall from innocence and the promise of redemption.

There are of course numerous particulars to support such an interpretation, and Professor Pearson and others have mustered them cogently; they need not be reviewed here. What does need to be said is commonplace enough: that the analogies Melville brings forward in support of his story—Billy as Adam, his hanging as a kind of Ascension, the yardarm as the True Cross, and so on—prove nothing in themselves about either his intention or his achievement. This is not simply because they are matched by an equal number of analogies of a quite different sort (so Billy, for example, is also compared to Apollo, to Hercules, to a Tahitian of Captain Cook's time courteously but indifferently receiving the ministrations of Christian missionaries, and to a St. Bernard dog). We are also to bear in mind that we are reading a nineteenth-century, not a seventeenth-century, writer; in Melville's time the literary apprehension of Christian myth was nearly as divorced from sacramental religion, and as merely moral and pathetic when not wholly sentimental, as the apprehension of classical myth. But in any case we need above all to look to the whole development of Melville's actual narrative and to the particular disposition and intensity of its insistences. The question is: how do all these evidences operate in the story? do they determine the action and constitute its first meaning? or are they at most a kind of illustrative commentary, suggesting by familiar analogy the appropriate pitch of feeling?

There is little doubt that Melville meant his story to be in some manner exemplary and that as he worked on it he found it profoundly moving; he "believed" in it. The strength of intimation in an inveterate explainer like Melville is in some proportion to the weight and spur of his own perplexities. The religious metaphors in *Billy Budd* do indeed confirm our sense of a religious depth in Melville's sensibility. But we must be wary of abstracting the stuff of these metaphors from his immediate deployment of them—the obvious temptation, but somehow especially insidious with this work. Melville himself is explicit about his procedures. Reaching the limit of observation and analysis in his presentation of John Claggart, he turns for a clinching notation to the Scriptural formula of the "mysteries of iniquity" (Chapter 12). Now what he was trying to express seems to me sufficiently identified in that precisely climactic phrase, which perfectly secures his idea of the "something defective and abnormal" in the constitution of the master-at-arms. But Melville himself recognized and characteristically specified the risk he was taking in thus falling back, here and elsewhere, on the "lexicon of Holy Writ" in an age which had grown indifferent to it, which could no longer be relied on to understand all that might be involved in it. His caution is itself pointedly cautionary. For our time is not so much skeptical of religious doctrines and symbols—certainly not passionately and burdensomely skeptical as Melville was—as it is ignorant of them, which Melville was not. Perhaps the first truth about us in this respect is that we are the embarrassed receivers of (in Carlo Levi's phrase) a civilization which used to be Christian. We respect, we are in a civil way habituated to, the positions of Christian belief; but the norms of our experience no longer reinforce them. And finding in a document like *Billy Budd* that this half-forgotten vocabulary has been restored to use, we may be overimpressed, mistaking mere unembarrassed familiarity with it for a reconstitution of its prime significance. But to make of *Billy Budd* an attempt, and an attempt comparable to Milton's, to reanimate the Christian myth of human destiny under divine law is to respond less to the limiting and authenticating particulars of Melville's story than to the pathos of its corroborative analogies and allusions, or perhaps to the transferred pathos of our own progressive disregard of them. Also it is to claim for Melville the kind of positive testament or settled belief which seems inconsistent with what we know of him; which all his tenacity in doubt, his frank and courageous ignorance, his respect for the discomforts of truth and the phenomenal ambiguities of existence, would have gone to keep him from taking refuge in, even for the space of a story, even at the end of his life.

No, the actual telling of *Billy Budd* will not bear so grand a burden of meaning, and was not intended to. What its limiting circumstances are, Melville is concerned to say as precisely as he can. His use of the military setting in constraint of the events of his story is to the point here. The martial law by which Billy goes to his death is usually held to be symbolic of some universal law or authority, such as divine providence: I think mistakenly. Nor can I follow Professor Richard Chase in comparing it with the "abstract legality" confronted by Antigone or the "inhumanly enforced legality" of *The Winter's Tale*; for the official agencies of justice in these plays are to be understood as wrong precisely in that, being "abstract" and "inhuman," they are other than what they ought to be. But Melville is at some pains to present the martial law as morally *sui generis*, and in its own terms morally unimpeachable. It is designed, he reminds us, solely to subserve the extraordinary circumstance of war. It is "War's child," as Captain Vere tells the court, and must of its nature look "but to the frontage, the appearance" of things—and not wrongly. As against moral or divine law it can have no regard to questions of motive or judgments of virtue: "The prisoner's deed—with that alone we have to do." It is for this terrible eventuality alone, otherwise it would be indefensible. But in the circumstances Melville sets out, there is no appeal from it.

Why Melville's story rides so easily in this rigid context, and what it gains from it, are absorbing questions, but beyond the compass of the present essay.[3] My point now is simply that in *Billy Budd* martial law and the "military necessity" are accepted in their own right, without ulterior design. Melville does not choose, as he did in *White-Jacket,* to judge the martial discipline by a higher moral law; he makes such a standard available neither to Vere and the court in their search for the right action (though they reach out to it) nor to the reader in judging what has happened. Christian conscience, mercy, the judgment of God—these are neither directly opposed to martial law nor put aside as meaningless. Melville has Vere speak of such considerations as having the force of "Nature" in the hearts of men but as being, in the "singular" given case, inapplicable. Doctrines of Christianity are invoked in full support of the pathos of the story, but assent to them is not what is at stake. It interested Melville, indeed it profoundly moved him, to point out in passing how one part of his narrative seemed to confirm the Calvinist doctrine of depravity or how another suggested the "heresy" of natural innocence, but these propositions are not, as such, his subject or argument. The whole movement of suggestion in Melville's narrative seems to me the reverse of allegorical;

[3] The search for answers might begin with Vigny's *Servitudes et Grandeurs Militaires* (1835), which provides, I think, a much truer parallel to *Billy Budd* than Milton's majestic poems. The resemblances are striking. Both Vigny and Melville (each having elsewhere, in *Stello* and *Pierre,* dramatized the Romantic theme of the suffering and heroism of the creative imagination) discovered in the action of obedience to martial discipline a more compelling occasion for moral drama; both responded to the resignation and self-effacement of military service as a more profoundly moving symbol of imaginable virtue. Indeed Vigny's notation of "a certain puerility" in the military character sheds light on a controversial aspect of the character of Billy Budd—as his treatment of Collingwood, in which we are asked specifically to apprehend "all that the sense of duty can subdue in a great soul," sheds light on Captain Vere. (Melville, we may note, had also paid his respects to Collingwood, and for the same reasons, in *White-Jacket.*)

Curiously it is Vigny's book which is the more didactic, being openly concerned to advance a general moral discipline for a post-Christian culture. "Is anything still sacred?" Vigny asked: "in the universal foundering of creeds, to what wreckage can brave hands still cleave?" His answer was that "creeds are weak, but man is strong," and he went on in his closing chapter to describe a "religion of Honor," which is characterized by "manly decency" and the "passive grandeur" of personal abnegation: "Whereas all other virtues seem to be sent down from Heaven to take us by the hand and raise us up, this alone appears to be innate and to be straining heavenwards. It is a wholly human virtue, born of the earth and earning no heavenly reward after death. It is indeed the virtue of the life of this world." The implicit logic of Melville's rendering of his two heroes could not be stated more sympathetically.

the words and names for the action of the story, the thoughts and analogies that help define it, follow from it and are subject to it. The image of the action itself, of a particular occurrence involving particular persons, stands first.

In *Billy Budd* this image is constituted first of all by the three main characters, and the action proceeds from the capacity of spirit painstakingly attributed to each of them. Each is set before us as a kind of natural force; in fact Melville's probing curiosity projects what might seem a thoroughly deterministic explanation of their behavior if it was not so clearly in the service of a stubborn and wondering sense of their free agency. "Character" is in general rather curiously exhibited here, Melville's language repeatedly suggesting that it is best apprehended at any given moment by a kind of *savoring*. A man's character derives from the accumulated conditions (the seasonings, so to speak) of his whole life, and so registers as a "taste" or "flavor" on the "moral palate," as though too subtly compounded for stricter definition. It may be that no sequence of dramatic events will wholly communicate this distinguishing savor of character; the necessities of action, in art as in life, show little enough respect for persons. But the mode of exposition Melville turned to has other resources than dramatization, other ways of declaring its meanings. So the climax of this minutely specifying narration is reached in an episode in which the actual event is withheld, and we are referred instead to the *character* of the participants.

This is the episode in which, the trial over, Vere privately tells Billy the court's decision. Given in very nearly the shortest chapter of the narrative (Chapter 23), it follows the longest and most detailed; and in contrast to the thorough exposition just concluded (of Vere's distress, the hesitant proceedings of the court, the ambiguities of the evidence, and all Vere's patient argument) it moves instead by conjecture and reticence. "Beyond the communication of the sentence," the main section of it begins, "what took place at this interview was never known." Yet on this elliptical passage the full weight of the narrative, accelerating after its slow-paced beginnings into the drama of the middle chapters, centers and falls, its steady simple movement coming full stop. By working so sensible a change of pace and manner, and by explicitly likening the hidden event to what must happen wherever in the world the circumstances are "at all akin to those here attempted to be set forth," Melville appears for the moment to be concentrating our attention on the very heart of his whole conception. What we are told is what it chiefly concerns him to have us know—the phenomenal quality of character in his two heroes. In their essential being Vere and Billy are as one, "each radically sharing in the rarer qualities of our nature—so rare indeed as to be all but incredible to average minds however much cultivated." On this basis and in these limited terms the narrator will risk "some conjectures." But insofar as his conjecture does accord with the rarity of spirit by which he has identified his protagonists, it may lead into the profoundest truth, it may be definitive.

So the chapter's central paragraph begins: "It would have been in consonance with the spirit of Captain Vere. . . ." The capacity of spirit being known, the weight and bearing of the event may be measured and its meaning grasped. And what capacity of spirit Melville meant to set before us begins to be confirmed in the virtues he gravely imagines as "not improbably" brought into play in the interview: in Vere, utter frankness and unselfishness, making him confess his own part in Billy's sentencing, and intensifying into the compassion of a father; in Billy an equal frankness, and bravery of course, but also joy, in the realization of his Captain's extraordinary trust. Yet these impressive virtues are in a way incidental. What draws the narrator on is the magnitude of the capability they speak for. Translated out of their customary stations, Vere and Billy meet as "two of great Nature's nobler order." Their entire competence of spirit before the event is assumed; only the immediate exercise of it goes past saying. Though the narration here makes a show of drawing back even from conjecture, the quality and the significance of the action continue to be defined; exact terms are used. Melville writes that "there is no telling the sacrament" when two such spirits embrace, but the very word "sacrament" precisely advances his explanation. The same tactic directs the closing sentence of this astonishing paragraph: "There is privacy at the time, inviolable to the survivor, and holy oblivion, the sequel to each diviner magnanimity, providentially covers all at last." Here again the withholding is according to the inmost nature of that which is being disclosed; the "privacy" of the scene is a consequence of the great and rare virtue, the "magnanimity," at work in it.[4]

May we not take this explanation, and the word that thus concludes it, as literally as we can? As with martial law, Melville's purpose was not to universalize the particular phenomenon, the capacity of spirit generating this encounter, but simply to identify it, to declare

[4] This view of what Melville was driving at in *Billy Budd,* and of his deliberateness in getting to it, is reinforced by examination of the manuscript drafts of this passage (in the Houghton Library, at Harvard). In its first form the paragraph is somewhat differently phrased; Vere and Billy are called simply "two of the nobler order," and the passage ends: "and holy oblivion the desirable thing for each diviner magnanimity, naturally ensues." Rewriting—his corrections are pencilled in—Melville brought into sharper focus the suggestion of "naturally" by crossing out the adverb itself but then enlarging the preceding phrase to "two of great Nature's nobler order." This allowed him to introduce a further perspective with "providentially," as if to call to mind that wider frame of being within which not only the life of man but the encompassing life of all creation is circumscribed. The change in the last clause corresponds. In speaking of what would be the "desirable thing," Melville

it in its own name. In Vere and Billy, the passage affirms, we have to do with magnanimity, with greatness of soul, a quality which, though "all but incredible to average minds however much cultivated," is nevertheless according to nature, and is touched with divinity—or whatever in human conduct is suggestive of divinity. Though it is constrained by Claggart's depravity of spirit (also "according to nature") and has still to undergo the pitiless operation of the "military necessity," this greatness of soul in the two heroes achieves in the sacrament of their coming together an "inviolable," a "diviner" magnanimity. As there is a mystery of iniquity in Claggart, there is a mystery of magnanimity in these two. It is given no power to prevent the now settled outcome of the action. Yet its radiance is beyond catastrophe. It is such as can survive those decisive accidents of individual existence—age, health, station, luck, particular experience—which Melville consistently presented the lives of his characters as being determined by. Now the narrative has come to its defining climax. Here the tone is set for what remains to be told, and not at the pitch of tragedy—the tone of exalted acceptance and muted patient joy which will be heard in the account of Billy in irons like a "slumbering child," in Billy's "God bless Captain Vere!" in Vere's dying with Billy's name on his lips (not in remorse, Melville specifies), and finally, and with what sure art, in the gravely acquiescent music of the closing ballad.

## III

This view of the action of *Billy Budd* (a view not discouraged by the dedication to the "great heart" of Jack Chase) does not, I think, deny the story any power of suggestion or degree of achievement. Perhaps it may remove the sense of disproportion between theme and occasion which Professor Pearson's and kindred readings leave us with, yet at the same time increase the interest of Melville's actual accomplishment. For an idea of some fulfilled greatness of soul lies, as we know, at the center not only of classical tradition in moral philosophy and literature but of Christian tradition as well. It lies also (as securely as ideas of equality and civil liberty) at the heart of the democratic ethos. The great-souled man—what significant reckoning of our duty and destiny, whether in the mode of tragedy or satire or prophecy or

---

had rounded off his idea too restrictively; with the apparently neutral word "sequel" he reached out past subjective wish to an indifferent order of nature and providence which to his imagination all human actions belong to and gain dignity from, and which an event so charged as this with emotion and with necessity would most vividly exemplify.

What he did not change is also significant. In both versions, it will be noticed, the center of gravity in the closing sentence is the same: "each diviner magnanimity."

simple witness, does not somehow take account of him? For what else do we especially revere a Washington and a Lincoln, whose unique place in the national pantheon is surely something more than the sum of their historical deeds? And what more momentous question can be put to the democratic writer than the question of greatness of mind and spirit in a mass society?

To follow out this view of the story might well lead into discussion of Melville's "Americanism," an absorbing matter certainly, though at present rather shopworn. Just as usefully it may lead us back to a parallel which I have made some point here of questioning—the example of Milton. The Milton who matters here, however, is not the Christian poet of paradise lost and regained but the prideful humanist whose dedication to the idea of magnanimity is proverbial in English letters. Milton's concern with this virtue in his writings, and his explicit pride in the pursuit of it in his life, are in fact foremost among the qualities which have given him his peculiar personal aura and earned him so much gratuitous personal hostility in our own antiheroic times. They are also of the essence of his Protestantism, and it is not likely to be altogether accidental that the two writers of epic imagination and enterprise in the Protestant camp (if we may imagine one) of Anglo-American literature should show a common concern, a considered preoccupation, with magnanimity.

As we might expect, Milton was confident and unembarrassed in deploying the term. He used it consistently and (according to his lights) precisely, to denote a summary condition of virtuousness in which the lesser particular virtues were gathered up and lifted to grandeur; in this he followed the Aristotelian definition of magnanimity as the "crowning ornament" of the virtuous character (*Nich. Ethics,* IV, iii, 16). What is especially Miltonic is his emphasis on rational self-consciousness in the exercise of magnanimity. For him the concept signifies the highest reach of that "pious and just honoring of ourselves" which is a duty of the virtuous man second only to love of God. Cultivation of magnanimity thus becomes the great end of education—so we find him saying in this famous and characteristic sentence: "I call therefore a compleat and generous Education that which fits a man to perform justly, skillfully, and magnanimously all the offices both private and public of Peace and War." But to describe the ideal education is to consider what end man was born for; and it is in the account of the creation of Adam that we come to the furthest reach of Milton's idea:

> There wanted yet the Master work, the end
> Of all yet don; a Creature who not prone
> And Brute as other Creatures, but endu'd
> With Sanctitie of Reason might erect

> His Stature, and upright with Front serene
> Govern the rest, self-knowing, and from thence
> Magnanimous to correspond with Heav'n. . . .

In magnanimity, so conceived, natural creation rises to its sovereign beauty and fulfillment. Would any nineteenth-century transcendentalist or mystical democrat ever claim more than this for the instructed soul of man?

Of these associations some were still viable for Melville but not all. It was precisely a doctrinal confidence in what the great-souled man might "correspond with" that, two hundred years later, his intelligence despaired of. At the same time certain outwardly passive virtues like humility and disinterestedness had come to seem far more positive and potentially heroic than they had been to Milton in his time. So Melville could specify in Vere a "certain unaffected modesty of manhood" without diminishing his general "ascendancy of character" or his Miltonic readiness for all private and public offices of peace and war. It is still, however, a traditionally heroic image of magnanimity that we are shown at the beginning of *Billy Budd* in the chapters on Nelson. Nelson's greatness in command is assumed; what concerned Melville was his personal behavior at Trafalgar and the charge of "vainglory" and "affectation" it lay open to. And though Melville was on the defensive here, he unequivocally championed the impulse of the great-hearted hero to display his greatness and love the glory of it. Given "a nature like Nelson" and the opportunity of a Trafalgar, then the "sort of priestly motive" that directed the great commander's conduct was, Melville insisted in one of his showiest sentences, altogether natural and fitting, coming from that "exaltation of sentiment" which is the mark of the truly heroic action.[5]

The point is not that Milton's conception of magnanimity is a "source" of *Billy Budd*. What we are considering is not a case of "influence" but a comparable turn and reach of mind, formed in a broadly common moral tradition though expressing very different stages in its devolution. To Milton magnanimity was within the achieving of every wise and good man, a condition of completed moral being to be reached through rational procedures of education and piety. To Melville it was a rarer thing—much less a condition to be achieved, much more a mysterious distillation of certain transactions and contingencies in certain men's lives. At the high tide of his creative energy he could imagine it as naturally resulting from that "unshackled,

[5] This defense of Nelson's love of glory, it may be noted, fits perfectly the Aristotelian concept of greatness of soul, according to which, "honor is the object with which the great-souled are concerned, since it is honor above all else which great men claim and deserve." Furthermore, "he that claims less than he deserves is small-souled. . . ." *Nich. Ethics,* IV, iii, 8 and 11.

democratic spirit of Christianity" in which America seemed destined to lead the world; we know how quickly this confidence went out of him. He found himself unable to assume even a moral efficacy in magnanimity, since he could not be sure in the first place of the moral order of creation, any more than he could have much faith in the moral justness of American society; both seemed paralyzingly indifferent to degrees of virtue. Nor could he take refuge in ideas of the infinitude of the private man or of the priesthood of the individual soul, as the simpler Protestant and democratic optimisms of his time would encourage him to. This being so, his undertaking in *Billy Budd*, and his success in it, are all the more impressive.

But did he in fact succeed? The character and role of Captain Vere fit well enough the traditional notion of magnanimity, but what about the character of Billy Budd? What has Miltonic magnanimity to do with the "mindless innocence" (as Professor Chase has put it) of the boy sailor? Given the character Melville presents, how much can be claimed for it? "To be nothing more than innocent!"—Claggart's "cynic disdain" may not be unreasonable; in one form or another it has been shared by most critics of the story. Have we not, in Billy, an expression of sentiment poignant in itself but unassimilated and unresolved in the narrative, and best explained (as Professor Chase would explain it) by the life-history and personal necessities of the author? [6]

But magnanimity, we may note again, is not a substantive virtue. No particular actions prove it or follow from it. What the word describes is a certain dimension of spirit which the virtuous man may rise to and which any moral event may conceivably participate in. Whatever has a soul (and to Melville's excruciating animism anything can seem to) may in certain extraordinary circumstances grow into the condition of magnanimity, the soul that is called innocent not less than the soul instructed by experience. If innocence is compatible with virtuousness—and in characterizing Billy, Melville did not doubt that it is: "a virtue went out of him"—then it too is capable of its own kind of magnanimity.

Here again we may appeal to Melville's care to be explicit; for in working out his conception of the character of Billy Budd—a "child-man" not incapable of moral reflection yet mysteriously uncorrupted, able to conceive of death but like a savage warrior "wholly without irrational fear of it"—Melville does in fact "denominate" it categorically. This is in a passage of explanation added to Chapter 16 of the revised draft, just after Billy has been approached by an apparent

[6] Richard Chase, "Introduction," *Selected Tales and Poems by Herman Melville* (New York, 1950), pp. xiii–xvi.

conspiracy of mutiny (though in his innocence he has hardly understood it as that). Melville, first specifying that the thought of reporting these overtures never entered Billy's mind, pushes on to a more positive claim, though at the moment a superfluous one: even if the step of reporting what he had heard *had* been suggested to him, "he would have been deterred from taking it by the thought, one of novice-magnanimity, that it would savor overmuch of the dirty work of a tell-tale." A special sort of magnanimity, awkwardly qualified and, though capable of choosing between evils, not yet decisively tested: nevertheless Melville makes it the defining motive in his conjecture here. Notice, too, that the term is introduced to attribute to Billy a natural revulsion from the role of informer; for in this he is sensibly at one with Captain Vere, who will respond to Claggart's accusations in the same way. To the magnanimous man, conscious of his nature and of the reputation it rightfully deserves, there may be a greater sin than breach of the ninth commandment but there is none more loathsome. It is a sudden intuition that Claggart is bearing false witness which goads Vere into the intemperate threat of the yard-arm-end, and so gives the master-at-arms his right to a full hearing; it is "horror" of his accuser, as against mere "amazement" at the accusation, that paralyzes Billy in Claggart's presence.

Can Melville's intention be doubted: to show Vere and Billy as bound to one another in a complementary greatness of soul? [7] As the story moves on to the music of its close we are shown how each in his own way has instructed the other; how, so to speak, the magnanimity possible to virtuous innocence has fulfilled itself and in turn given its mysterious blessing to the world-sustaining magnanimity of experienced and commissioned virtue. The first represents that part of man which, being born to nature, remains of nature; the second represents that part of man which is uniquely of his own making, his defining burden as a moral and historical creature. Melville is explicit about what has happened. The "tension of agony" in Billy, he wrote, "survived not the something healing in the closeted interview with Captain Vere"; in turn Billy, restored to the role of "peacemaker," has lifted Vere, for all his anguish, beyond remorse. The motions of magnanimity

[7] The question of Billy's moral nature, and its progress through the story, may need a few words more. At several points in the narrative Melville takes time to describe the exact blend of character in Billy as it affects the action then going forward; each time he shows Billy occupied in positive moral considerations (Chapters 17, 22, 25). In Chapters 25 and 26 it is suggested that Billy has undergone a degree of visible (or only just not invisible) change as a result of his "tension of agony." His "rare personal beauty" is "spiritualized," the skull begins "delicately to be defined" beneath the skin. But these suggestions are muted and unforced. An allegorical demonstration of the progress of the soul does not seem intended. By way of contrast, think how Hawthorne might have handled this action; did handle it, in fact, in *The Marble Faun.*

under the most agonizing worldly duress: that is Melville's image and his theme.

By way of elaboration, we have been shown three fulfillments of human nature—on one side depravity (or "monomania," his word for Claggart as for Ahab), on the other these two forms of magnanimity self-realized through recognition of one another. No exact balance is struck. We sense some division of intention or disequilibrium. Midway in the story, for example, it is the conflict between the two sides that engrosses interest, or the attack of the one upon the other. But in the slowdown Claggart is not allowed to be any real match for the other two,[8] and we see that Melville's most profound intention lies further along. It is seldom observed how pitiable Claggart is, in a way in which Billy and Vere are not. Once acting in the open he cannot really deceive the Captain or leave any lasting scar on Billy—though his own understrappers deceive him at will (Chapter 14), as indeed he deceives himself; it is not usually pointed out that Claggart believes his absurd accusation. He is envious and despairing, an embodiment of those life-denying "sins refined" which in *Clarel* were Melville's vision of Sodom and Gomorrah. But he is not a hypocrite (as was Bland, the master-at-arms of *White-Jacket*). In such a nature, Melville made a point of explaining, conscience functions not in restraint of its terrible determinations but as their helpless agent. Also it is not usually observed how abruptly and entirely Claggart and what is embodied in him are dismissed from the story. After the trial he is barely mentioned again; no trace of his concerted malignity is allowed to survive the interview between Vere and Billy. It is as though Melville's conception of the radically opposing crystallizations possible to human nature—confidence and envy, love and hate, frankness and dissimulation, assurance and despair, magnanimity and depravity—had swung clear of his tormenting search for belief, so that he was free to rise at the climax of his story to a different and surer theme: the conjunction of the two magnanimities, making sacrifice to the military necessity.

"The only great ones among mankind are the poet, the priest, and the soldier; the man who sings, the man who blesses, and the man who sacrifices, and sacrifices himself." It is not, I think, the grand design of Christian myth nor the example of Greek tragedy or Miltonic epic but this confessional aphorism of Baudelaire's that stands nearest the logic and authority of *Billy Budd*.[9] Strong judgments of life-in-general, of good and evil and law and justice, may throb through Mel-

[8] Another of Melville's revisions is worth noting in this respect. Describing Claggart's response to "the moral phenomenon presented in Billy Budd" (Chapter 13), he struck out this too schematic remark: "In him he recognized his own direct opposite. . . ."

[9] *Mon Coeur Mis à Nu*, No. 48.

ville's narrative, but its work is not to prove them. It asks not, "what is life?" or "what are the ways of God?" or even "what is justice?" but, "given this imaginable event in these circumstances, what power of response is there in certain phenomenal men?" So we are shown one kind of greatness of spirit in Vere, the soldier–priest of the military necessity, joining with another kind in Billy Budd, whose power to bless transfigures not only his own life. We observe, as in Baudelaire's journal or Vigny's *Servitudes et Grandeurs Militaires,* how an apprehension of the moral chaos and inscrutability of the experienced world has been held in balance by an austere intuition of honor and of personal abnegation. Yet for all their poignancy the specific terms of Melville's narrative do not require our option. Far less than in *Moby-Dick* or *Pierre* or *The Confidence-Man* or even *White-Jacket* are we asked to subscribe to some world-view. This is only a story, a narrative of "what befell" certain men in the year of the Great Mutiny. What does require our option, however, is the manner of the telling, the compassion and patiently exact utterance of the writer who has "sung" the story; for it is through these that we are brought to "believe" in the degree of virtue claimed for its protagonists.

"What one notices in him," E. M. Forster said of the Melville of *Billy Budd,* "is that his apprehensions are free from personal worry." [10] His imagination and compassion work immediately, taking fair and full measure of their impressive objects. This cannot be said of all of Melville's work, in much of which (most damagingly in *Pierre*) all we can clearly see at times are the features of his own discomposure. And given the circumstances of the writing of *Billy Budd*—his career as an author of books thirty years behind him, his life closing down, his own two boys dead and his old energies gone—we might reasonably expect incoherence, failure of control. Instead we find a concentration, and integrity, of performance that match the best in his earlier career. The achievement, and the act of mind it speaks for, are indeed extraordinary. The particulars of this story positively invited misconstruction, as they still invite misinterpretation. Straining after dramatic effect or insistence on an allegorical lesson could only have diminished its grave authority. Mere indignation or pity would have left it no more than a parable of injustice, an exercise in resentment. But there is no indignation or outrage in the telling of *Billy Budd*—no quarrel at all, with God or society or law or nature or any agency of human suffering. Rather there is a poise and sureness of judgment (but at no loss of the appetite for explanation); a compassionate objectivity which, claiming no credit for itself, keeps its fine temper before the worst appearances; most of all, a readiness of apprehension possible

[10] *Aspects of the Novel,* p. 206.

only to an actual, measurable greatness of mind. That is to say, there is intellectual magnanimity—which Milton proposed in his treatise on Christian doctrine as the greatest of that "first class of special virtues connected with the duty of man towards himself."

This is the example the Melville of *Billy Budd* offers as a writer. A personal example, of course, but also a formal example, and of the most radical sort—as Henry James would remind us in declaring that "the deepest quality of a work of art will always be the quality of the mind of the producer." If we add that this quality does not come full-blown into the world but must be made and exercised, like any rational creation, then we may at least imagine how Melville's still barely tapped capacity to "influence" might yet be productively exploited, and his legacy as a writer husbanded and renewed.

# Two Inside Narratives: *Billy Budd* and *L'Étranger*

### *by Roger Shattuck*

It is here that Melville's cryptic and cautionary subtitle, *An Inside Narrative,* takes on significance for both novels. Applied in the present context to Camus's novel, it appropriately calls attention to the deepest movement of the book's action: a human consciousness undergoing mitosis, an inner division experienced very late by a physically mature man. We witness the process from inside through the ambiguous and shifting use of a double *je*. Meursault's final self-affirmation as a condemned man is a truly heroic effort to bring the parts back together in defiance of society's judgment and of Christian forgiveness.

Meursault's separation from himself and return, sighted through Melville's complementary action, allows fresh insight into the character structure of *Billy Budd.* Billy never comes unstuck from himself because he already belongs to a larger division. In Melville's story we are symbolically carried inside the microcosm of one individual broken into three parts: Captain Vere standing for the pride of both reason and authority, Claggart, who represents "depravity according to nature," and Billy, who embodies ingenuous goodness. None of the three is pure, and none is a whole man. *The Indomitable* puts to sea less as the ship of state or society than as the ship of a complex individual. Under the stress of social and political upheaval lengthily described in the opening chapters, this living unit, this multiple man sacrifices one part of himself in order to maintain discipline. The whole pulse of the novel implies that such a sacrifice must be lethal. *Billy Budd* is anything but a "testament of acceptance," as it has often been described since E. L. G. Watson's article in 1933.[1] Nor is it (as it

---

*"Two Inside Narratives:* Billy Budd *and* L'Étranger" *by Roger Shattuck. From* Texas Studies in Literature and Language *4 (Autumn 1962): 318–20.* 

[1] *New England Quarterly,* VI (June, 1933), 319–327. [See this volume, p. 11.]

has been labelled by an eloquent lecturer for a society working to abolish the institution) the only novel ever written in defense of capital punishment. In unmistakable allegory Melville presents the possibility of man's inward division and the accompanying dangers of self-destruction.

Held up together to the light, these two novels have an iridescent quality, a flickering of implied meanings ranging from Christian atonement, to the embodiment of fate in social situations, to the sinfulness of God himself. Despite flaws of artificial style and some labored symbolism in both books, they are true gems with the capacity to refract light in multiple ways. But the clearest beam they transmit when set in the proper alignment emanates from a single area of experience. These two inside narratives reveal man's consciousness deadlocked with its own most awe-inspiring work—civilization—here in the form of "justice" under law. The particular natures of Billy and Meursault lead to exceptional treatments of this theme, faced less squarely and less often in fiction than we should like to believe.

We have come to think of the novel as the exhibiting of a hero constantly testing, risking, and extending himself in some form of play-acting inspired by the realization of being alive: Robinson Crusoe to Rastignac to Proust's Marcel. Stendhal's most characteristic creations prove themselves in moments of intense crisis by their ability to improvise both action and emotion. In novels so markedly different as those of D. H. Lawrence and Virginia Woolf, the heroes, after first ascertaining the strictures of life around them, begin to recast their inner being in response to glimpsed possibilities of experience. But the two heroes we have been examining refuse to engage in this energetic psychological prospecting in the face of the "forms" of civilized existence. Billy never deviates from his given character and has no qualms about himself. True, he fears a flogging and is stunned by his impulsive violence; but he sleeps soundly the night before his execution. Meursault, just a few degrees more sophisticated than Billy, begins in a comparable state of mind, is then wrenched far enough out of this restricted sensibility to see himself as others see him, goes on to refuse that knowledge in the scene with the chaplain, and at the end reasserts his original "simple" consciousness of himself as a man. Thus they both stubbornly remain on a level with the *mécanique* of justice that condemns them and do not evade it by any subtle psychological contortion.

In an era of post-Freudian plastic surgery of the soul, it is this flat-footedness of character that gives the two books their archaic tone and haunting appeal. Billy's final blessing and Meursault's final curse grow out of the same primitive moral awareness of how man has constructed around himself the potential instrument of his own destruction. Melville and Camus do not squander their distress on the future of civilization. They know that in the struggle to live with it and ahead of it, it is the self that suffers and the self that may perish. Save him.

# The Passion of Billy Budd

*by W. H. Auden*

If, when we finish reading *Billy Budd,* we are left with questions which we feel have been raised but not answered, if so to speak the equation has not come out to a finite number, as in a work of art it should, this is not due to any lack of talent on Melville's part, but to the insolubility of the religious paradox in aesthetic terms.

For any writer who attempts a portrait of the Christ-like is faced with the following problems. His central figure

a) must be innocent of sin, yet a man like us in all things tempted as we are if he is given any aesthetic advantages, he at once ceases to be the God–Man and becomes the Man–God, the Aesthetic Hero, Hercules, who must be admired, but cannot be imitated. His sinlessness must be the result of faith, not of fortune.
b) He must be shown as failing in a worldy sense, i.e., as coming into collision with the law of this world, otherwise there is no proof that his sinlessness is due, not to faith, but to mere worldly prudence.
c) Failure and suffering, however, are in themselves no proof of faith, because the collision with the law may equally well be the result of pride and sin. The crucified Christ is flanked by two crucified thieves.
d) The suffering must at one and the same time be willed and not-willed. If it seems entirely against the will of the sufferer, he becomes pathetic, if it seems entirely brought about by his own actions, he becomes tragic, and it is impossible to distinguish between pride and faith as the cause of his suffering.

His ironically comic approach solved all the problems, I think, except the last one. As long as Don Quixote is mad, the suffering is not quite real, but if he becomes sane and still resists he becomes tragically proud.

Melville, on the other hand, solves this problem. The Passion of Billy Budd is convincing, but fails in respects where Cervantes succeeds, and the ways in which he fails are interesting for the light they

---

*"The Passion of Billy Budd." From* The Enchafèd Flood *by W. H. Auden (New York: Random House, Inc., 1950), pp. 144–49.* 

throw on the romantic conception of life. Like many other romantics Melville seems to hold:

1) That innocence and sinlessness are identical, or rather perhaps that only the innocent, i.e., those who have never known the law, can be sinless. Once a man becomes conscious, he becomes a sinner. As long as he is not conscious of guilt, what he does is not sin. This is to push St. Paul's remark "Except I had known the Law, I had not known sin" still further to mean that "Except I had known sin, I would not have sinned."[1] Thus when Billy Budd first appears he is the Prelapsarian Adam:

> Billy Budd in many respects was little more than a sort of upright barbarian, much such perhaps as Adam presumably might have been ere the urbane Serpent wriggled himself into his company.

He may have done things which in a conscious person would be sin —there appears to have been a certain Bristol Molly—but he feels no guilt.

2) That the unconscious and innocent are marked by great physical beauty, and therefore that the beautiful are sinless. This is true for Billy Budd as it was for Bulkington and Queequeg.

If the story were to be simply the story of the Fall, i.e., the story of how the Devil (Claggart) tempted Adam (Budd) into the knowledge of good and evil, this would not matter, but Melville wants Budd also to be the Second Adam, the sinless victim who suffers voluntarily for the sins of the whole world. But in order to be that he must know what sin is, or else his suffering is not redemptive, but only one more sin on our part. Further, as long as Billy Budd is only the Prelapsarian Adam, our nostalgic image of what we would still be if we had not fallen, his beauty is a perfectly adequate symbol but the moment he becomes the Second Adam, the saving example whom we all should follow, this beauty becomes an illegitimate aesthetic advantage. The flaw of the stammer will not quite do, for this is only an aesthetic weakness, not a deliberate abandonment of advantages. It succeeds in making Billy Budd the innocent who "as a sheep before the shearer is dumb so openeth he not his mouth," but it makes his dumbness against his will not with it. We can never look like that, any more than, once we have become conscious, we can go back to unconsciousness, so how can we imitate his example? He becomes an aesthetic hero to admire

[1] In the Barrister's dream in *The Hunting of the Snark* the pig is charged with deserting its sty, i.e., the crime is not the eating of the tree but the expulsion from Eden. The Snark who is officially the counsel for the defence is also the accuser–judge and the sentence is a repetition of the offence. "Transportation for life."

from a distance. Melville seems to have been aware that something must happen to Billy to change him from the unconscious Adam into the conscious Christ but, in terms of his fable, he cannot make this explicit and the decisive transition has to take place off-stage in the final interview between Billy and Captain Vere.

## *Claggart*

Similar insoluble paradoxes are raised by the demonic, the religious passion in reverse. For the demonic must be moved solely by pride, just as the religious must be moved solely by faith and love. Absolute pride cannot be manifested aesthetically because it tolerates no weakness except itself which thinks of itself as absolute strength.

Absolute pride denies that the six other deadly sins are its children and despises them as weakness, being incapable of seeing that it is the source of all weakness. The Devil, therefore, cannot himself be lustful, gluttonous, avaricious, envious, slothful, or angry, for his pride will not allow him to be anything less than proud. He can only pretend in disguise to be any of these without actually feeling them; he can only "act" them. His acts must appear to be arbitrary and quite motiveless. No accurate aesthetic portrayal, therefore, is possible; Iago has to be given some motive, yet if the motive is convincing, he ceases to be demonic.

So with Claggart. Just as the bias in Melville's treatment of Billy Budd is a tendency to identify consciousness and sin, so he makes Claggart identify innocence with love; "To be nothing more than innocent," he sneers on seeing Billy Budd. This is no doubt what the serpent says to Adam, but it is not what he says to himself, which is rather "To be nothing more than loving." For the difference between God and the Devil is not that God does not know the meaning of good and evil and that the Devil does, but that God loves and the Devil will not love. That is why the motive for Claggart's behaviour, half-stated only to be withdrawn because no motive will really do, is homosexual desire.

In *Moby Dick,* where Ahab's pride revolts against lack of absolute strength, against being finite and dependent, the sexual symbolism centres round incest and the Oedipus situation, because incest is the magic act of self-derivation, self-autonomy, with the annihilation of all rival power.

In *Billy Budd,* the opposition is not strength/weakness, but innocence/guilt-consciousness, i.e., Claggart wishes to annihilate the difference either by becoming innocent himself or by acquiring an accomplice in guilt. If this is expressed sexually, the magic act must necessarily be homosexual, for the wish is for identity in innocence or in guilt, and identity demands the same sex.[2]

Claggart, as the Devil, cannot, of course, admit a sexual desire, for that would be an admission of loneliness which pride cannot admit. Either he must corrupt innocence through an underling or if that is not possible he must annihilate it, which he does.

[2] It is not an accident that many homosexuals should show a special preference for sailors, for the sailor on shore is symbolically the innocent god from the sea who is not bound by the law of the land and can therefore do anything without guilt. Indeed, in a book like Genet's *Querelle de Brest,* the hero is at once god and devil. He is adored because, though he is a murderer and a police informer and sexually promiscuous in every sense, though, that is, he loves no one but himself, is, in fact, Judas, yet he remains Billy Budd, the beautiful god who feels neither guilt nor remorse, and whose very crimes, therefore, are a proof of his divinity.

# Herman Melville

*by Albert Camus*

In the days when the whalers of Nantucket stayed at sea for several years, the young Melville, aged 22, took ship on one of them, then changed to a man-of-war and sailed the seas. On his return to America, he enjoyed a certain success with his traveller's tales, and then published his great books in the midst of indifference and incomprehension.[1] After the publication and failure of *The Confidence Man* (1857), Melville, discouraged, "consents to annihilation." Having become a customs officer and the father of a family, he entered into an almost complete silence (a few poems, very infrequently) which was to last thirty years. He then hastened to write a masterpiece, *Billy Budd* (completed in April 1891), and died, a few months later, forgotten (a three-line obituary in the *New York Times*). He had to wait until our own day for America and Europe finally to give him his place, among the greatest geniuses of the West.

It is scarcely easier to speak in a few pages of a work which has the tumultuous dimensions of the oceans where it was born than to summarize the Bible or condense Shakespeare. But to judge Melville's genius, if nothing else, we must recognize that his works depict a spiritual experience of unequalled intensity, and that they are to some extent symbolic. Certain critics[2] have discussed this obvious fact, which now scarcely seems open to doubt. His admirable books are numbered among those exceptional works that can be read in different ways, which are at one and the same time both obvious and obscure, as dark as the noonday sun and yet as clear as deep water. The wise man and the child can both draw sustenance from them. The story of Captain Ahab, for example, flying from the Southern to the Northern

---



[1] For a long time, *Moby Dick* was considered as an adventure story suitable as a school prize.

[2] Let me, in passing, advise critics to read page 449 of *Mardi* in the French translation.

seas in pursuit of Moby Dick, the white whale who has taken off his leg, can doubtless be read as the fatal passion of a character driven mad by grief and loneliness. But it can also be seen as one of the most overwhelming myths ever invented on the subject of the struggle of man against evil, depicting the irresistible logic which finally leads the just man to take up arms first against creation and the creator, then against his fellows and against himself.[3] Let us have no doubt about it: if it is true that talent recreates life while genius has the additional gift of crowning it with myths, Melville is first and foremost a creator of myths.

I will add that these myths, contrary to what people say of them, are clear. They are obscure only in so far as the root of all suffering and all greatness lies buried in the darkness of the earth. They are no more obscure than Phèdre's cries, Hamlet's silences, or the triumphant songs of Don Giovanni. It seems to me, on the contrary (and this would deserve detailed development), that Melville never wrote anything but the same book, which he began again and again. This single book is the story of a voyage, inspired first of all solely by the joyful curiosity of youth (*Typee, Omoo,* etc.), then later inhabited by an increasingly wild and burning anguish. *Mardi* is the first, magnificent story in which Melville declares that this quest, which nothing can appease, and in which, finally, "pursuers and pursued fly across a boundless ocean," now lies open. It is in this work that Melville becomes aware of the fascinating call which for ever echoes within him: "I have undertaken a journey without maps." And again: "I am the restless hunter, the one who has no home." *Moby Dick* simply carries to perfection the great themes of *Mardi*. But since artistic perfection is also inadequate to quench the kind of thirst with which we are confronted here, Melville will start once again, in *Pierre or Ambiguities,* this unsuccessful masterpiece, to depict the quest of genius and misfortune whose sneering failure he will consecrate in the course of a long journey on the Mississippi which forms the theme of *The Confidence Man*.

This constantly rewritten book, this unwearying peregrination in the archipelago of dreams and bodies, on the ocean, "of which each wave is a soul," this Odyssey beneath an empty sky, make Melville into the Homer of the Pacific. But we must immediately add that, with him, Ulysses never returns to Ithaca. The country in which Melville weighs anchor with *Billy Budd* is a desert island. By allowing the young sailor, a figure of beauty and innocence, and whom he himself dearly loves, to be condemned to death, Captain Vere submits his heart to the law. And at the same time, by this flawless story which can be placed

[3] As an indication, here are some of the obviously symbolic pages of *Moby Dick* (French translation, Gallimard): pp. 120, 121, 123, 139, 173, 177, 191–3, 203, 209, 241, 310, 313, 339, 373, 415, 421, 452, 457, 460, 472, 485, 499, 503, 517, 520, 522.

on the same level as certain Greek tragedies, Melville tells us, in his old age, of his acceptance that beauty and innocence should be put to death so that an order may be maintained, and the ship of men continue to move forward towards an unknown horizon. Has he then truly secured the peace and final dwelling place which he nevertheless said could not be found in the Mardi archipelago? Or are we, on the contrary, faced with this final shipwreck that Melville in his despair asked of the gods? "One cannot blaspheme and live," he had proclaimed. At the height of consent, is not *Billy Budd* the highest blasphemy? This can never be known, any more than whether Melville did finally consent to a terrible order, or whether, in quest of the spirit, he allowed himself to be led, as he had asked, "beyond the reefs, in sunless seas, into night and death." But no one, in any case, measuring the long anguish which runs through his life and work, will fail to acknowledge the greatness, all the more anguished in being the fruit of self-conquest, of the reply which he has given.

But this, though it had to be said, should mislead no one as to the true genius of Melville and the sovereignty of his art. It is bursting with health, strength, upsurges of humour, and human laughter. It was not he who opened the shop of sombre allegories which today enchant our sad Europe. As a creator, he is for example at the farthest possible remove from Kafka, and he makes us aware of this writer's artistic limitations. However irreplaceable it may be, the spiritual experience in Kafka's work overflows the modes of expression and invention, which remain monotonous. In Melville, this experience is balanced by expression and invention, and constantly finds its flesh and blood in them. Like the greatest artists, Melville constructed his symbols out of concrete things, not from the material of dreams. The creator of myths partakes of genius only in so far as he inscribes these myths in the denseness of reality, and not in the fleeting clouds of the imagination. In Kafka, the reality which he describes is created by the symbol, the fact stems from the image, whereas in Melville the symbol emerges from reality, the image is born of what we see with our own eyes.[4] This is why Melville never cut himself off from flesh or nature, which are barely perceptible in Kafka's work. On the contrary, Melville's lyricism, which reminds us of Shakespeare's, makes use of the four elements. He mingles the Bible with the sea, the music of the waves with that of the spheres, the poetry of the days with the grandeur of the Atlantic. He is inexhaustible, like the winds which blow for thousands of miles across empty oceans and which, when they reach

[4] In Melville, the metaphor suggests the dream, but from a concrete, physical starting point. In *Mardi,* for example, the hero comes across "huts of flame." However, they are made of red tropical creepers, whose leaves had happened to be raised up by the wind.

the coast, still have strength enough to destroy whole villages. He rages, like Lear's madness, over the wild seas where Moby Dick and the spirit of evil crouch among the waves. When the storm and total destruction have passed, a strange calm rises from the primitive waters, the silent pity which transfigures tragedies. Above the speechless crew, the perfect body of Billy Budd turns gently at the end of its rope in the pink and grey light of the approaching day.

T. E. Lawrence placed *Moby Dick* by the side of *The Possessed* or *War and Peace*. One can, without hesitation, place by its side *Billy Budd, Mardi, Benito Cereno,* and some others. These anguished books, which describe the destruction of man, but in which life is exalted on each page, are inexhaustible sources of strength and pity. We find in them revolt and acceptance, unconquerable and endless love, passion for beauty, language of the highest order, in short, genius. "To perpetuate one's name," said Melville, "one must carve it on a heavy stone and sink it to the depths of the sea: depths last longer than heights." Depths do in fact have their painful virtue, as did the unjust silence in which Melville lived and died, and as did the ageless ocean which he unceasingly ploughed. From their endless darkness he one day drew his works, those visages of foam and night, carved by the waters, whose mysterious royalty has scarcely begun to shine upon us. Yet it already helps us to emerge effortlessly from our continent of shades and go once more down to the sea, towards its light and secret.

PART TWO

# *View Points*

## *Leon Howard*

*Billy Budd, Foretopman* differs from Melville's earlier novels because it was a mature and successfully controlled outgrowth of the inquisitiveness about human behavior which made *Clarel* so remarkable. It developed out of one of his experiments in combining prose and verse, such as the one he published as "John Marr"—an introductory sketch of a remarkably handsome young sailor who was condemned to be hanged as the ringleader of an incipient mutiny and who expressed his last sentiments in a ballad composed on the eve of the execution. But Billy, as he crept into Melville's imagination with all the physical signs of noble birth, seems to have been difficult to sketch. He appears to have first been imagined as guilty and then as innocent of the charge, and the conception of innocence was the germ from which the story grew. Why should an innocent man be hanged? The best inference to be drawn from the surviving working manuscript is that Melville's first impulse was to answer that he was a victim of another man's wickedness. He had personally known, if the record of *White Jacket* can be trusted, a ship's master-at-arms with an evil sadistic genius beneath a bland exterior, and he was acutely aware of the power for evil that a malicious person in such a position might possess. Out of his memory and still-indignant awareness he created the character of John Claggart who was to accuse the innocent Billy of a crime and be killed by a spontaneous blow from the speechless sailor. And for this, under the Articles of War, Billy had to be hanged.

Yet Melville had learned that the world was far too complex to be pictured in black and white. Evil and goodness might exist side by side, as he made clear in the almost allegorical exaggeration of these qualities in Claggart and Billy, but reality was in between. Billy had not struck "through the mask" of anything (as Ahab had tried to do) by hitting Claggart. Justice was not absolute, as Pierre had believed, but man-made. Billy had to be hanged not as a matter of course but by decision of court-martial. And Melville also had within his experience a court-martial such as Billy would have had to endure: his cousin,

---

*From* Herman Melville *by Leon Howard, University of Minnesota Pamphlets on American Writers, 13 (Minneapolis: University of Minnesota Press, 1961): 42–44.* 

Guert Gansevoort, had presided over such a one under the direction of Captain Alexander Mackenzie of the brig *Somers* in 1842 and had hanged the son of the secretary of war on a similar charge. The affair had created a scandal which was being revived at the time Melville was working on the *Billy Budd* manuscript and it was still a family mystery that Guert should have been almost broken by his action while insisting that it "was *approved* of God." Here was a mystery that appealed to the mature Melville more than the mystery of Iago.

So, as his manuscript went through its various later stages of painful revision, he created the character of Captain Vere, master of H.M.S. *Indomitable* (or *Bellipotent,* as he finally decided to call it) during the Napoleonic wars, who resembled both Guert Gansevoort and Captain Mackenzie and was a wise and good man who loved Billy as a son but forced a reluctant court to condemn him to death. He talked privately with Billy to such effect that Billy died with the words "God bless Captain Vere" on his lips. But the captain was not blessed. He was haunted. He himself died murmuring the words—though not in accents of remorse—"Billy Budd, Billy Budd."

*Billy Budd* has almost as many meanings to as many readers as *Moby Dick,* and perhaps for the same reasons. It has the hidden ambivalence of any work of art which grows by accretion rather than by design, the ambiguity that is found in any intelligent and honest attempt to solve a profound problem of human behavior, and the power which an author only manages to get into a book when he succeeds in capturing in his own person the major tensions of his age. For the problem that bothered Melville in *Billy Budd* was not the problem of knowledge that had worried him in his youth. It was the problem of man. Is he a social being, responsible to the welfare of the society to which he belongs? Or is he an independent moral individual, responsible to his private awareness of guilt and innocence? This was the dilemma Captain Vere faced when, in Melville's fiction, the preservation of discipline in the British fleet was absolutely requisite to the preservation of England's freedom. Melville's solution was to make him behave as a social being but pay a penalty by suffering the private agonies of his private conscience.

The problem, however, was not a fictitious one. When Melville finished the last revision of his manuscript, on April 19, five months before his death in 1891, society had become far more complex than it had been when he dealt with the validity of individual awareness in *Moby Dick* forty years before. *Billy Budd* was not to be published until 1924, many years after its author's death. But the problem with which it dealt has not lessened with the passing years. Man's relationship to his private self and to the society in which he dwells is still the greatest source of tension of modern times. And Herman Melville's strongest claim to greatness is that his imaginative development kept abreast of the times—despite neglect and adversity and more than one failure, the acuteness and depth of his sensitivity never failed.

## *Ray B. West, Jr.*

. . . Where then does truth lie?

The answer, of course, is inherent in the novel itself. As is so often the case, however, Melville had considered the problem explicitly in *Clarel*:

> *Suppose an instituted creed*
> *(or truth or fable) should indeed*
> *To ashes fall; the spirit exhales,*
> *But reinfunds in active forms:*
> *Verse, popular verse, it charms or warms—*
> *Bellies philosophy's flattened sails—*
> *Tinctures the very book, perchance,*
> *Which claims arrest of its advance.*
>
> (XV, p. 105)

Here is an almost exact duplication of the situation in *Billy Budd.* Christianity and all it implies has fallen into decay. The spirit exhales, but only momentarily, awaiting the propitious moment again to belly philosophy's sails. Billy's act of innocent heroism supplies the opportunity—creates the situation. Authoritarianism and a changing concept of man's individual worth had conspired to bring about the destruction of the old gods. Billy's act (and by extension, Christ's) is seen more as tragic circumstance than as actual atonement. From Billy's act then springs the new myth, sung to the tune of a simple sailors' ballad. It is "verse, popular verse" which bellies the sails, which supplies the common man with a means of confronting the facts, not only of Billy's death, but of his own. It is not orthodox Christianity. It is not popular science. It is the simple creative act which pierces the mask of falsehood and error, which sees man's existence as an heroic submission to fate, but which is in constant rebellion against those forms which result in man's injustice to man.

If it seems odd that so apparent and so integrated a theme should have been missed by so many readers, the fact of its having been missed is only additional evidence of the difficulty which the modern reader

---

*From "The Unity of Billy Budd" by Ray B. West, Jr.,* Hudson Review *5 (Spring 1952): 126–27.* 

has with the ironic style in which *Billy Budd* is composed. The difficulty is multiplied in this case, because Melville did not employ (indeed, could not have employed) the lyric–ironic style of *Moby Dick,* to which we have, after a lapse of many years, become accustomed. Accompanying the positive theme of man's rejuvenation through myth, there is also, as we have indicated, the negative one of modern man's situation in an over-materialistic society: "atheized into a smatterer." In a satiric–ironic manner, Melville pretends to adopt the very style of the popular-prose writer against whom his book is at least partially directed. Despite the fact that his central theme betrays his principal intention—he had elsewhere written, "It is not the purpose of literature to purvey news",—he pretended to have written a story which, as he says, "has less to do with fable than with fact." He speaks of digressions and ragged edges, as though the very essence of truth lay in its absence of form. He pretends, in other words, to have written the very book which claims arrest of the advance of truth, or fable, or of instituted creeds; but the theme itself, the form which he has created in *Billy Budd,* tinctures the very book which he pretends to have written—the book of factual information concerning a mutiny at sea.

Contrary to current critical opinion, then, *Billy Budd* as a unified work not only is not marred by digressions and irrelevancies, it is a triumph of architectonic structure. When Melville protests that as a writer of "facts" he is prevented from achieving "an architectural finial," he is merely calling attention (in a method not uncommon in literature) to his central theme, which is in fact presented as an architectural finial, since it lies imbedded in the popular ballad "Billy in the Darbies," which ends the book.

*But they'll lash me in hammock, drop me deep.*
*Fathoms down, fathoms down, how I'll dream fast asleep.*
*I feel it stealing now. Sentry, are you there?*
*Just ease these darbies at the wrist,*
*And roll me over fair.*
*I am sleepy, and the oozy weeds about me twist.*

This is not great poetry, but it was not intended to be. Neither is it, as one critic calls it, doggerel. It is intended merely to represent the primitive, but universal, ability of man to temper the harsh facts of death, to come to terms with nature, through art. It represents Melville's final expression of faith in mankind—faith in the ability of the common man to see beyond the misrepresentations of evil, however disguised; faith that the essential beauty and heroism of man will always be recognized and celebrated in artistic form, however crude.

*Billy Budd* is not in itself a tragedy, although it is an expression of belief in the tragic predicament of man. If we need distinguish it by supplying a name, I would suggest that it be called satiric-allegory. It does not pretend to the organ voice of *Moby Dick.* It combines the biting irony of Swiftian satire with the lyric hopefulness of John Bunyan. That it has been so little understood need not finally surprise us when we consider the history of Melville's literary career from *Mardi* onward. Among other things, *Billy Budd* suggests the possibility that Melville believed the rich tongue of Shakespeare (the use of which he borrowed in *Moby Dick* and *Pierre*) to be as obsolete as the scarlet and gold of Lord Nelson's office. Perhaps this is why he chose to write otherwise in his final work.

## *Quentin Anderson*

Through a process I do not understand, Melville had, in the intervening years, come to abate his exorbitant claim on life. (*Israel Potter* gives an intimation that he had done so through sinking his claim in the generic demand life makes on death, and reflecting that we are all, in the end, equally deprived. But this, though it may be true, seems too thin to be useful.) However one may choose to account for the fact, *Billy Budd* is informed not by luminous commonplaces but by a sort of primal moral wonder.

Perhaps no work usually called a novel has as little of the novelistic intention as this one. Kafka and Trollope picking their way down the scaffold of social circumstance are closer to one another than either is to the Melville of this story. That the world should be multifarious and odd, and yet shot through with causes, and histories which have beginnings, middles and ends—this is the wonder which animates the novelist, but the wonder that Melville feels and expresses through Claggart, Budd and Vere is primal in that although it comes after experience it seems to look back to what has conditioned experience since birth. (The same kind of wonder and the same impulse to celebrate the literally awful are present in the last poems of Yeats.) A naturalistic account of the grounds of this wonder is possible, but irrelevant to Melville's aim. That there should be men and women, fathers, mothers, sons and daughters is no doubt enough to account for what Melville wanted to say, for the mind pauses and retreats in awe before these ultimate differences and likenesses if they are once seen in their primal aspect. Good and evil are terms in which we express our conviction as to the way we have discharged the offices which

---

have been allotted to us in this constellation of relationships, and our imaginations tend to parcel out the world (quite without distinction as to what lies without and what within) into these provinces of responsibility, just as the Greeks gave each god a realm in which to perform those tasks which defined him.

In this spirit Melville approached his own nature in *Billy Budd,* asking how, so to speak, Bottom could play all these parts, but never doubting that he did. How could innocence, malignity and righteousness be housed in the soul? The book does not and could not contain an answer. Its theological references are designed to reinforce the wonder, never to lessen or dispel it. Christian doctrines are but the tropes of Melville's total feeling.

This third voice in Melville's work is to be distinguished from that of *Pierre* and *The Confidence Man* and from that of *Moby-Dick* and *Benito Cereno.* It may sound in the late poetry, but in Melville's prose it seems to be confined to *Billy Budd.* We tend to ignore the precise and fiery passions of old age (as we used to ignore those of children), apparently feeling that a deep engagement in life recedes as inevitably as the tide. Yeats and Melville show the depth of our error.

## *Joseph Schiffman*

Billy's last words, "God bless Captain Vere," have been taken by almost all critics to be Melville's last words, words of accommodation, resignation, his last whispered "acceptance" of the realities of life. Mumford, for example, says: "At last he [Melville] was reconciled . . . [he found] the ultimate peace of resignation. . . . As Melville's own end approached, he cried out with Billy Budd: God bless Captain Vere!" [1]

The disillusioned of the world toasted Melville as a long-unclaimed member of their heartbroken family. Here indeed was a prize recruit —Melville, the rebel who had questioned "the inalienable right to property, the dogmas of democracy, the righteousness of imperialist wars and Christian missions . . . [who] dared to discuss in a voice louder than a whisper such horrific subjects as cannibalism, venereal disease and polygamy . . ." [2] had, in the ripe wisdom of old age, uttered "God

---

*From "Melville's Final Stage, Irony: A Re-Examination of* Billy Budd *Criticism" by Joseph Schiffman,* American Literature *22 (May, 1950): 129–30.* 

[1] Lewis Mumford, *Herman Melville* (New York, 1929), p. 357.

[2] From Willard Thorp's Introduction to *Herman Melville, Representative Selections* (New York, 1938), p. xcvii.

bless Captain Vere," thereby accepting authority. A prize catch indeed, if it were really so!

E. L. Grant Watson tips his hat to the Melville of *Billy Budd*:

> Melville [he says] is no longer a rebel. It should be noted that Billy Budd has not, even under the severest provocation, any element of rebellion in him; he is too free a soul [this man with the rope around his neck] *to need a quality which is a virtue only in slaves.* . . . Billy Budd is marked by this *supreme quality of acceptance.* . . . [Melville's] philosophy in it has *grown* from that of rebellion to . . . acceptance. . . .[3]

Watson's bias towards a philosophy of acceptance is clear; he searches in Melville for confirmation of his own dogma.

Charles Weir, Jr., makes much of the "God bless Captain Vere" scene, accepting it at face value. He says: "The paradox has been established: injustice [the hanging of Billy] may find its place within the pattern of a larger all-embracing divine righteousness." [4] What this all-embracing divine righteousness may be is not specified. Is Vere God? Or is he, as he himself very clearly sets forth, the agent of the King? If the latter, then Billy is the unhappy pawn in a game he never understood, aristocratic England versus democratic France.

Both Watson and Weir warn the reader that Melville must be plumbed and probed if he is to surrender his secrets. Watson says, "The critic's function is rather to hint at what lies beneath—hidden, sometimes, under the surface." [5] Weir warns that, "in writing *Billy Budd* Melville had a deeper intent than that of simply telling a story." [6] And yet Watson and Weir ignore their own good advice, for in propounding their theory of Melville's "acceptance," they do not probe beneath Billy's last words. They accept "God bless Captain Vere" as the denouement of the tale, its final judgment, as the ripe wisdom of a tired Melville come to terms with life.[7]

These critics, it seems to me, commit three basic mistakes in their attempt at divining Melville's final moments of thought in his story. First, they divorce *Billy Budd* from all of Melville's other works in the way that a man might search for roots in treetops. Second, they isolate Melville from the Gilded Age, the time in which Melville produced

[3] E. L. Grant Watson, "Melville's Testament of Acceptance," *New England Quarterly,* VI, 319–327 (June, 1933) (italics mine). [See this volume, p. 11.]

[4] Charles Weir, Jr., "Malice Reconciled: A Note on Melville's Billy Budd," *University of Toronto Quarterly,* XIII, 276–285 (April, 1944).

[5] Watson, *op. cit.*, p. 321.

[6] Weir, *op. cit.*, p. 280.

[7] The fullest treatment of the theory of Melville's "acceptance" can be found in William Ellery Sedgwick, *Herman Melville: The Tragedy of Mind* (Cambridge, Mass., 1945), pp. 231–249. Thorp agrees with Sedgwick. He says: "With good reason, *Billy Budd* has been called 'Melville's testament of acceptance . . .' " (*Literary History of the United States,* New York, 1948, I, 469).

*Billy Budd.*[8] Third, and most important, they accept at face value the words "God bless Captain Vere," forgetting that Melville is always something other than obvious.

## *Lawrance Thompson*

The manuscript of *Billy Budd* shows that at one time Melville had thought to conclude with an abstract generalization which would group the major characters, antithetically, in terms of their emblematic values, thus:

"Here ends a story not unwarranted by what sometimes happens in this incomprehensible world of ours—Innocence and infamy, *spiritual depravity* [italics added] and fair repute."

The two contrasting allegorical implications of the passage provide a suitable summary of Melville's artistic methods and thematic concerns. In terms of that allegorical meaning which would satisfy the orthodox Christian reader, the emblematic correlations are clear: Billy Budd represents innocence, and Claggart represents infamy; Claggart represents depravity and Billy Budd represents fair repute. However, in terms of that sinister allegorical meaning which better satisfied Melville, the emblematic correlations are far more involved. Once over lightly: Billy Budd represents innocence again, Claggart represents infamy again; but Captain Vere picks up the other two values and shares them both with Claggart. Take it through again, in part: Claggart is certainly emblematic of infamy and depravity, and even in certain quarters and at certain times (with the early Billy Budd, for example), Claggart would seem emblematic of fair repute. But Claggart plays a kind of confidence-man game with Billy Budd, in order to seduce him; furthermore, be it remembered, it was Captain Vere himself who looked on Claggart the informer and remembered that he was the Captain's "own subordinate and charged among other things with police surveillance." By emblematic and allegorical extension, Claggart is an agent of Vere, an agent of God. His powers are permissive, even as Satan's powers are permissive in Christian theological dogma. By extension, then, Claggart and Vere do indeed share the infamy and depravity, but only through the permissive will of the "Maker of All

---

*From* Melville's Quarrel with God *by Lawrance Thompson (Princeton, N. J.: Princeton University Press, Princeton Paperbacks, 1952), pp. 412–14.* 

[8] F. O. Matthiessen is the only critic to my knowledge who has attempted to place Melville in the context of the Gilded Age, that most disastrous of periods for the serious American writer. See Matthiessen, *American Renaissance* (New York, 1946), pp. 513–514.

that is Fair." Who is to blame? On whom does the ultimate responsibility rest? Who is the Original Sinner? The answer is made clear by the allegorical narrative. Yet the ultimate irony of that answer, for Melville, would seem to be that the Guilty One should so largely manage to conceal His depravity behind a mask of fair repute. What kind of depravity? Natural? Melville wrote, "Spiritual depravity."

In conclusion, we may ask again how it is possible that anyone who has read *Billy Budd* carefully could ever describe it as Melville's "Testament of Acceptance." But we know the answer to that: Melville cunningly arranged to have certain kinds of readers arrive at exactly that mistaken interpretation. Artistically and thematically, then, *Billy Budd* is cut from the same piece of cloth (a dark sort of spiritual sailcloth) which supplied the makings for *White-Jacket, Moby-Dick, Pierre, The Confidence-Man*. No doubt Hawthorne was right in saying that Melville could never be comfortable in his unbelief; no doubt but that Melville's wistfulness for belief had much to do with making him so furiously resentful (even jealous) toward Christian believers; furiously angry with God for being God, and for robbing him of belief. Motivated by his mingled disillusionment, hate, skepticism, agnosticism, wistfulness, Melville projected his complex narratives not merely because he was caught on the horns of what some like to view as a profoundly ambiguous paradox but also because he took comfort and delight in employing ambiguities and equivocations as stylistic devices for hoodwinking and deceiving those readers whom he hated because they would be inclined to resent the dark implications of his single thematic concern. His obsession, which remained quite constant, achieved an increasingly Schopenhauerish intensity of hate toward the end of his life. On the last page of the manuscript of *Billy Budd* he wrote, "END OF BOOK April 19th, 1891." He died on September 28, 1891.

## *Richard Chase*

The real theme of *Billy Budd* is castration and cannibalism, the ritual murder and eating of the Host. During his trial Billy proclaims his faithfulness to the king and to Captain Vere by saying, "I have eaten the King's bread, and I am true to the King." When, "without remorse," the dying Captain Vere murmurs, "Billy Budd, Billy Budd," he expresses faithfulness, dependence, and longing. He had eaten of the Host, and he was true to the Host. After forty years Melville had

---

*From* Herman Melville *by Richard Chase (New York: The Macmillan Company, 1949), p. 269.* 

returned to the theme of *Typee.* In that book the young hero had extricated himself from the valley by a sudden exchange of passivity for action. Billy Budd is fatally passive, his acts of violence being unconsciously calculated to ensure his final submission. All of Billy's conscious acts are toward passivity, the first one being his quick acquiescence in his impressment, an act which causes the hero-worshiping sailors to regard him with "surprise" and "silent reproach." In symbolic language, Billy Budd is seeking his own castration—seeking to yield up his vitality to an authoritative but kindly father, whom he finds in Captain Vere.

## *E. M. Forster*

*Billy Budd* is a remote unearthly episode, but it is a song not without words, and should be read both for its own beauty and as an introduction to more difficult works. Evil is labelled and personified instead of slipping over the ocean and round the world, and Melville's mind can be observed more easily. What one notices in him is that his apprehensions are free from personal worry, so that we become bigger not smaller after sharing them. . . . Melville—after the initial roughness of his realism—reaches straight back into the universal, to a blackness and sadness so transcending our own that they are indistinguishable from glory. He says, "In certain moods no man can weigh this world without throwing in something somehow like Original Sin to strike the uneven balance." He threw it in, that undefinable something, the balance righted itself, and he gave us harmony and temporary salvation.

## *Thomas Woodson*

Finally, it seems fair to compare Thoreau's Brown, his last portrait of magnanimity, with Melville's last such character, Billy Budd. Billy shares with Brown the legendary qualities of the American magnanimous hero. He is poor, simple, and uneducated, but is a prince in

---

*From* Aspects of the Novel *by E. M. Forster (London: Edward Arnold, Ltd.; New York: Harcourt, Brace and World, 1927), p. 184.* 

*From "Thoreau on Poverty and Magnanimity" by Thomas Woodson,* PMLA *85 (January 1970): 34.* 

disguise, the royal foundling whose heroic form can be seen by those who know how to look. Billy's story is an "inside narrative," but its public counterpart is the life and death of Lord Nelson, whose "excessive love of glory" (p. 58)[1] qualifies him as an Aristotelian *megalopsuchos*. Billy the "child–man" (p. 86) is an "angel of God" (p. 101), a Hercules (p. 51), a young Achilles (p. 71); he is also the embodiment of democratic innocence and defenselessness, the impressed sailor. Billy dies, as did Brown, by peremptory hanging, punished for committing the murder of a purely evil force which bore false witness to the possibilities of life, just as Brown was punished. Melville even compares Billy's arm, which speaks for him in striking Claggart, to "the flame from a discharged cannon at night" (p. 99). But of course the characters are vastly different; Billy retains his innocence to the moment of death, while Brown resisted at Harpers Ferry with a cool and implacable fury, over the bodies of his dead and dying sons. At the moment of death, Billy dares to bless, while Brown dares only to curse.

Melville speaks of magnanimity, but in a way Thoreau would not have understood in October 1859. It is in his relation to Captain Vere after the murder that Billy's "novice magnanimity" (p. 85) becomes a "diviner magnanimity" (p. 115), and what Werner Berthoff has described as "the mystery of magnanimity," the complementary greatness of soul" of judge and criminal, even for a moment the love of father and son, of Abraham and Isaac.[2] For Melville, as for Thoreau, anything which has a soul may grow into the condition of magnanimity, but Melville's understanding of democratic characterization moves beyond the simplistic, abstracting polemics to which the ugly fact of slavery reduced Thoreau.

## *M. L. Rosenthal and A. J. M. Smith*

This monologue, in addition to what it tells us of Billy's character, becomes, indirectly, something more—a humble, loving but fatalistic view of the world. Through the doomed sailor's thoughts, first of all, we receive a picture of the good life as one in which a few creature-comforts would be available and in which men would judge each other's motives genially and affectionately. Even if he has some "bad"

---

*From M. L. Rosenthal and A. J. M. Smith,* Exploring Poetry *(New York: The Macmillan Company, 1955), pp. 374–75.* 

[1] *Citations in the text are from Herman Melville,* Billy Budd, Sailor (An Inside Narrative), *ed. Harrison Hayford and Merton M. Sealts, Jr. (Chicago, 1962).*

[2] Billy Budd, Sailor, *p. 115. Werner Berthoff,* The Example of Melville *(Princeton, 1962), pp. 193–200.* [See this volume, p. 67.]

thoughts, Billy's mind does not rest with them. It passes sadly over to details of his coming execution, halts momentarily with the all-too-answerable question "But aren't it all sham?"—but finally moves to calm acceptance of his lot. He knows, as a matter of fact, that it *is* "all sham," that the laws of society have arbitrarily made him the scapegoat in a ritual-travesty of justice which he does not quite understand. But although he could not at first imagine his own death, he at last comes to see himself as already, literally, dead: "I am sleepy, and the oozy weeds about me twist."

As so often happens, in the dramatic monologue and in other kinds of poetry as well, the "story" here involves a projection into the future: first a recognition that a change must come about and a parallel tension at the prospect (as in Billy's inability to get his imagination fastened on the precise fact of his own physical death), then the realization of its full meaning, and finally the crystallization of an attitude or insight (in this case, Billy's complete acceptance of his future condition).

*We* too must "accept." We must accept the truth of this projection of imagination. We shall do so if we feel that we know the speaker's essential character, if the progression of his thoughts and feelings is credible, and if the external objects he observes and the way they enter his consciousness are acutely enough conceived. In such case, the "meanings" the monologue carries along with it will be seen as having their own truth and life and will exercise a certain power over us whether we are prepared to believe in them generally or not. Artifice and realism move together in Melville's poem to bring this conviction about in us. Every reader separately will have come to his own conclusion, of course, about the degree of psychological realism present in Billy's thinking. But realism is not in any case the only consideration, for the phrasing and the balanced movements of the poem are not always of the kind one would expect in a simple, untutored person like Billy. There are humble picturings—"down on his marrow-bones," "a nibble-bit o' biscuit," and "a blur's in my eyes." And there are others with the poet's own trademark on them —"the moon-shine astray," "a jewel-block they'll make of me," "pendent pearl from the yard-arm-end," "his cheek . . . like the budding pink." There is a rough correspondence between the alternation of the two kinds of language and the swinging, up–down movements of the physical visualization in this poem. The chaplain goes *down* on his knees; the moon comes *up* and then, in forecast, *down;* Billy imagines himself *up* in the air, then *down* to the moment before he is *raised* to be hanged; and so on until the movement is quieted in his vision of himself *sinking* and, finally, rocking slowly at the *bottom* of the sea. Through much of the monologue, the sense of emotional depression grows deeper the more clearly Billy visualizes his coming death. Yet the closing lines, with their steadily downward movement until they reach a point of final rest at the ocean-bottom, actually represent a heightening of his morale as his agitation of spirit subsides and he moves into total acceptance. The poet behind the scenes—somewhat like a theatrical director—has been experimentally manipulating basic dramatic feeling toward this final impression. To do so, he has had to distort nature and add something to it. Without such distortions and additions, however, poetry and the other arts would lose their inner truthfulness to the felt meaning of experience.

## *Helen Pinkerton*

Though slander struck him when he knew no guilt,
His anger made the slander true. Vere saw
With equal grief his death and perfect guilt
And could not love, like Billy, perfect law.

## *W. H. Auden*

Towards the end he sailed into an extraordinary mildness,
And anchored in his home and reached his wife
And rode within the harbour of her hand,
And went across each morning to an office
As though his occupation were another island.

Goodness existed: that was the new knowledge
His terror had to blow itself quite out
To let him see it; but it was the gale had blown him
Past the Cape Horn of sensible success
Which cries: "This rock is Eden. Shipwreck here."

But deafened him with thunder and confused with lightning:
—The maniac hero hunting like a jewel
The rare ambiguous monster that had maimed his sex,
Hatred for hatred ending in a scream,

---

*"Billy Budd" by Helen Pinkerton,* Southern Review *4 (Summer 1968): 717.* 

*"Herman Melville" by W. H. Auden. From* Collected Shorter Poems 1927–1957 *by W. H. Auden (New York: Random House, Inc., 1940), pp. 146–47.* 

The unexplained survivor breaking off the nightmare—
All that was intricate and false; the truth was simple.

Evil is unspectacular and always human,
And shares our bed and eats at our own table,
And we are introduced to Goodness very day,
Even in drawing-rooms among a crowd of faults;
He has a name like Billy and is almost perfect
But wears a stammer like a decoration:
And every time they meet the same thing has to happen;
It is the Evil that is helpless like a lover
And has to pick a quarrel and succeeds,
And both are openly destroyed before our eyes.

For now he was awake and knew
No one is ever spared except in dreams;
But there was something else the nightmare had distorted—
Even the punishment was human and a form of love:
The howling storm had been his father's presence
And all the time he had been carried on his father's breast.

Who now had set him gently down and left him.
He stood upon the narrow balcony and listened:
And all the stars above him sang as in his childhood
"All, all is vanity," but it was not the same;
For now the words descended like the calm of mountains—
—Nathaniel had been shy because his love was selfish—
But now he cried in exultation and surrender
"The Godhead is broken like bread. We are the pieces."

And sat down at his desk and wrote a story.

# *Chronology of Important Dates*

| | *Melville* | *The Age* |
|---|---|---|
| 1819 | 1 August born in New York City, third child of Allan and Maria Gansevoort Melville. | Washington Irving's *The Sketch Book of Geoffrey Crayon, Gent.* |
| 1820 | | Missouri Compromise. |
| 1821 | | James Fenimore Cooper, *The Spy.* |
| 1824 | | Oregon trail opened as a trade route. |
| 1826 | | American Lyceum movement started. Cooper, *Last of the Mohicans.* |
| 1829 | | Construction started on Baltimore and Ohio Railroad. |
| 1830 | Family moves to Albany where, two years later, Allan M. dies following derangement and subsequent bankruptcy. Melville then for seven years tries various jobs | |
| 1831 | | Anti-Slavery League founded. |
| 1832 | | First Clipper ship launched, in Baltimore. |
| 1836 | | Emerson, *Nature*. Transcendental club meetings. |
| 1839 | Sails as crew member of merchant ship *St. Lawrence,* whence later (1849) his book *Redburn.* | |
| 1841 | 3 January ships from Fairhaven (New Bedford) on whaleship *Acushnet* to South Seas. | |
| 1842 | With Richard Greene jumps ship and flees to Typee valley on the Marquesan Island of | Society Islands taken over by France. |

| | | |
|---|---|---|
| | Nukahiva, where lives for short time, whence the substance of *Typee* (1846). About July leaves Typee on whaleship *Lucy Ann,* arriving soon after at Tahiti, where he rebels with other crew members, is imprisoned for period in Papeete, but escapes and ships on whaleship *Charles and Henry.* | |
| 1843–44 | Works at pickup jobs in Honolulu, until enlists as ordinary seaman on board the frigate *United States,* for return to United States. This experience substantial part of his fifth book, *White-Jacket.* Discharged October 1844 in Boston. | |
| 1845–49 | Busy writing (see books above) and add, 1849, *Mardi.* Marries Elizabeth Shaw, daughter of Chief Justice Lemuel Shaw. Settles in New York City. | |
| 1846 | | War with Mexico. |
| 1849 | | California Gold Rush. |
| 1850 | Moves to Pittsfield, Massachusetts, buys farm called Arrowhead, and begins writing of "a whaling voyage." August 4 meets Hawthorne, to whom a year later he dedicates his rewritten and enlarged and deepened whaling voyage, now become *Moby-Dick.* | |
| 1851 | *Moby-Dick* published 18 October as *The Whale,* then in November in United States as *Moby-Dick.* For next four years pursues career of author, with *Pierre* (1852), short stories in magazines, many gathered in *Piazza Tales* (1856), *Israel Potter* (1855) and ending a great burst of creative energy, with *The Confidence-Man* (1857). | |

| | | |
|---|---|---|
| 1858 | | Lincoln–Douglas debates. |
| 1859 | | Discovery of oil, Titusville, Pennsylvania. Darwin, *Origin of the Species.* |
| 1860 | | Lincoln made president, War Between the States started. |
| 1863 | Moves back to New York City, 104 East 26 Street. | |
| 1865 | | Lee surrenders to Grant at Appomattox. Lincoln assassinated. |
| 1866 | *Battle Pieces* published in August; 5 December takes oath of office as Inspector of Customs at the Port of New York. | |
| 1871 | | Tweed Ring exposed in New York. Twain's *Gilded Age* published two years later. |
| 1876 | 3 June *Clarel* published at uncle Peter Gansevoort's expense. | |
| 1886 | 1 January retires from post in Customs House. Son Stanwix dies in San Francisco, 23 February. Is writing poetry. | |
| 1888 | 7 September *John Marr and Other Sailors* privately printed; 16 November begins work on *Billy Budd.* | |
| 1890 | | United States Census: population 62,979,766. Closing of frontier. |
| 1891 | *Timoleon* privately printed. *Billy Budd* completed (?) 19 April; 28 September dies in New York City; 1 October funeral at family residence, buried in Woodlawn Cemetery. | |

## *Notes on the Editor and Contributors*

HOWARD P. VINCENT, Professor of English at Kent State University, is the editor of the "Collected Poems of Herman Melville," co-editor of *Moby-Dick,* and author of many articles about American and British writers.

QUENTIN ANDERSON, Professor of English at Columbia University, has edited stories and novels by Henry James and Nathaniel Hawthorne. He is a frequent contributor to reviews and journals.

W. H. AUDEN, the Anglo-American poet, is connected with Melville through his brilliant study entitled *The Enchafèd Flood.*

WERNER BERTHOFF, Professor of English at Harvard University, is the author of *The Example of Melville.*

PAUL BRODTKORB, Assistant Professor of English at Hunter College, is the author of *Melville's White World.*

ALBERT CAMUS received the Nobel Prize for Literature and was the author of novels not needing citation here.

RICHARD CHASE was the author of a number of studies of American writers including one on Herman Melville.

RICHARD HARTER FOGLE, Professor at the University of North Carolina, is the author of books on Keats, Hawthorne, Melville, and Coleridge.

E. M. FORSTER, distinguished novelist who is best known for *A Passage to India,* died June 7, 1970.

LEON HOWARD, Professor of English at the University of California at Los Angeles, is the author of *The Connecticut Wits* and studies on Melville.

EUGENIO MONTALE is one of the most distinguished literary men of modern Italy.

HELEN PINKERTON teaches English at Stanford University.

CHARLES A. REICH, Professor of Law at Harvard University, is the author of *The Greening of America.*

EDWARD ROSENBERRY is Chairman of the Department of English at the University of Delaware and author of *Melville and the Comic Spirit.*

M. L. ROSENTHAL, Professor of English at New York University, was poetry editor of *The Nation* and is the author of *Modern Poets: A Critical Introduction.*

JOHN SEELYE, Professor of English at the University of Connecticut, has written *The Ironic Diagram; A Study of Melville.*

JOSEPH SCHIFFMAN, Professor of English and Chairman of the Department of English at Dickinson College, Carlisle, Pennsylvania, is editor of various works on American literature.

ROGER SHATTUCK, Professor of French and Italian at the University of Texas, is the author of *The Banquet Years.*

A. J. M. SMITH is Professor of English at Michigan State University and an anthologist of poetry.

LAWRANCE THOMPSON, Professor of English at Princeton University, is the author of a biography of Robert Frost.

WILLIAM YORK TINDALL, Professor Emeritus of English at Columbia University, has published a number of books on modern British literature.

E. L. GRANT WATSON is a practicing psychotherapist and the author of *The Mystery of Physical Life.*

RAY B. WEST, JR., Professor of English at San Francisco State College, was an editor of the *Western Review* and has published much on American literature.

THOMAS WOODSON, Associate Professor of English at The Ohio State University, is the editor of *Twentieth Century Interpretations of The Fall of the House of Usher,* and the author of articles on Melville, Thoreau, and Robert Lowell.

# *Selected Bibliography*

Anderson, Charles R., "The Genesis of *Billy Budd,*" *American Literature,* XII (November, 1940), 329–46.

Hayford, Harrison and Merton M. Sealts, Jr., eds., *Billy Budd, Sailor* (University of Chicago Press, 1962). An indispensable edition.

Matthiessen, F. O., *American Renaissance* (London, 1941). Important.

Pearson, Norman Holmes, "*Billy Budd:* 'The King's Yarn,'" *American Quarterly,* III (Summer 1951), 99–114.

Rathbun, John W., "*Billy Budd* and the Limits of Perception," *Nineteenth-Century Fiction,* XX (June 1965), 19–34.

Shulman, Robert, "Melville's 'Timoleon': From Plutarch to the Early Stages of *Billy Budd,*" *Comparative Literature,* XVI (Fall 1967), 351–61.

Stein, William Bysshe, "'Billy Budd': The Nightmare of History," *Criticism,* III (Summer 1961), 237–50.

Wagner, Vernon, "Billy Budd as Moby Dick: An Alternative Reading," in A. Dayle Wallace and Woodburn O. Ross, eds., *Studies in Honor of John Wilcox* (Detroit: Wayne State University Press, 1958), pp. 157–74.

Widmer, Kingsley, "The Perplexed Myths of Melville: *Billy Budd, Sailor,*" *PMLA, LXXXII* (October, 1967), 370–76.

Withim, Philip, "*Billy Budd:* Testament of Resistance," *Modern Language Quarterly,* XX (June, 1959), 115–27.

Zink, Karl E., "Herman Melville and the Forms—Irony and Social Criticisms in 'Billy Budd,' " *Accent,* XII (Summer 1952), 131–39.

# TWENTIETH CENTURY INTERPRETATIONS

MAYNARD MACK, *Series Editor*
Yale University

NOW AVAILABLE
*Collections of Critical Essays*
ON

ADVENTURES OF HUCKLEBERRY FINN
ALL FOR LOVE
THE AMBASSADORS
ARROWSMITH
AS YOU LIKE IT
BILLY BUDD
BLEAK HOUSE
THE BOOK OF JOB
BOSWELL'S LIFE OF JOHNSON
THE CASTLE
CORIOLANUS
DOCTOR FAUSTUS
DON JUAN
DUBLINERS
THE DUCHESS OF MALFI
ENDGAME
EURIPIDES' ALCESTIS
THE EVE OF ST. AGNES
THE FALL OF THE HOUSE OF USHER
A FAREWELL TO ARMS
THE FROGS
GRAY'S ELEGY
THE GREAT GATSBY
GULLIVER'S TRAVELS
HAMLET
HARD TIMES
HENRY IV, PART ONE
HENRY IV, PART TWO
HENRY IV

(*continued on next page*)

(*continued from previous page*)

The Iceman Cometh
Invisible Man
Julius Caesar
Keats's Odes
Light in August
Lord Jim
Major Barbara
Measure for Measure
The Merchant of Venice
Miss Lonelyhearts
Molloy, Malone Dies, the Unnamable
Moll Flanders
Much Ado About Nothing
The Nigger of the Narcissus
Oedipus Rex
The Old Man and the Sea
Pamela
A passage to India
The Playboy of the Western World
The Portrait of a Lady
A Portrait of the Artist as a Young Man
The Praise of Folly
Pride and Prejudice
The Rape of the Lock
The Rime of the Ancient Mariner
Robinson Crusoe
Romeo and Juliet
Samson Agonistes
The Scarlet Letter
Sir Gawain and the Green Knight
Songs of Innocence and of Experience
Sons and Lovers
The Sound and the Fury
The Tempest
Tess of the D'Urbervilles
Tom Jones
To the Lighthouse
The Turn of the Screw and Other Tales
Twelfth Night
Utopia
Vanity Fair
Walden
The Waste Land
Women in Love
Wuthering Heights

# TWENTIETH CENTURY VIEWS

## American Authors

S-TC-3 ROBERT FROST, edited by James M. Cox
S-TC-5 WHITMAN, edited by Roy Harvey Pearce
S-TC-6 SINCLAIR LEWIS, edited by Mark Schorer
S-TC-8 HEMINGWAY, edited by Robert P. Weeks
S-TC-10 THOREAU, edited by Sherman Paul
S-TC-12 EMERSON, edited by Milton R. Konvitz and Stephen E. Whicher
S-TC-13 MELVILLE, edited by Richard Chase
S-TC-20 EDITH WHARTON, edited by Irving Howe
S-TC-27 F. SCOTT FITZGERALD, edited by Arthur Mizener
S-TC-28 EMILY DICKINSON, edited by Richard B. Sewell
S-TC-29 EZRA POUND, edited by Walter Sutton
S-TC-30 MARK TWAIN, edited by Henry Nash Smith
S-TC-33 WALLACE STEVENS, edited by Marie Borroff
S-TC-34 HENRY JAMES, edited by Leon Edel
S-TC-38 AUDEN, edited by Monroe K. Spears
S-TC-39 O'NEILL, edited by John Gassner
S-TC-55 HAWTHORNE, edited by A. N. Kaul
S-TC-61 W. C. WILLIAMS, edited by J. Hillis Miller
S-TC-63 POE, edited by Robert Regen
S-TC-65 FAULKNER, edited by Robert Penn Warren
S-TC-66 STEPHEN CRANE, edited by Maurice Bassan
S-TC-69 MODERN AMERICAN THEATER, edited by Alvin B. Kernan
S-TC-79 ROBERT LOWELL, edited by Thomas Parkinson
S-TC-84 ARTHUR MILLER, edited by Robert W. Corrigan
S-TC-86 MARIANNE MOORE, edited by Charles Tomlinson

# TWENTIETH CENTURY VIEWS

## British Authors

S-TC-26 Jane Austen, edited by Ian Watt
S-TC-82 The Beowulf Poet, edited by Donald K. Fry
S-TC-58 Blake, edited by Northrop Frye
S-TC-31 Byron, edited by Paul West
S-TC-70 Coleridge, edited by Kathleen Coburn
S-TC-53 Conrad, edited by Marvin Mudrick
S-TC-72 Dickens, edited by Martin Price
S-TC-19 John Donne, edited by Helen Gardner
S-TC-32 Dryden, edited by Bernard N. Schilling
S-TC-90 George Eliot, edited by George R. Creeger
S-TC-2 T. S. Eliot, edited by Hugh Kenner
S-TC-9 Fielding, edited by Ronald Paulson
S-TC-59 Forster, edited by Malcolm Bradbury
S-TC-25 Hardy, edited by Albert Guérard
S-TC-57 Hopkins, edited by Geoffrey H. Hartman
S-TC-83 A. E. Housman, edited by Christopher Ricks
S-TC-48 Samuel Johnson, edited by Donald J. Greene
S-TC-22 Ben Jonson, edited by Jonas A. Barish
S-TC-43 Keats, edited by Walter Jackson Bate
S-TC-24 D. H. Lawrence, edited by Mark Spilka
S-TC-44 Marlowe, edited by Clifford Leech
S-TC-81 Andrew Marvell, edited by George deF. Lord
S-TC-60 Milton, edited by Louis L. Martz
S-TC-74 Modern British Dramatists, edited by John Russell Brown
S-TC-64 Restoration Dramatists, edited by Earl Miner
S-TC-85 Samuel Richardson, edited by John Carroll
S-TC-47 Shakespeare: The Comedies, edited by Kenneth Muir
S-TC-45 Shakespeare: The Histories, edited by Eugene M. Waith
S-TC-40 Shakespeare: The Tragedies, edited by Alfred Harbage
S-TC-50 G. B. Shaw, edited by R. J. Kaufmann
S-TC-49 Shelley, edited by George M. Ridenour
S-TC-80 Spenser, edited by Harry Berger, Jr.
S-TC-77 Laurence Sterne, edited by John Traugott
S-TC-35 Swift, edited by Ernest Tuveson
S-TC-75 Thackeray, edited by Alexander Welsh
S-TC-56 Dylan Thomas, edited by Charles B. Cox
S-TC-87 Oscar Wilde, edited by Richard Ellmann
S-TC-23 Yeats, edited by John Unterecker